D1045583

"Branding is a powerful force in the world of busine̶s̶s̶ ̶a̶n̶d̶ ̶h̶a̶s̶ ̶g̶r̶o̶w̶n̶ ̶i̶n̶ ̶i̶m̶p̶o̶r̶-
tance over time. I have spent my life developing brands and I have found that
my business brands can not be separated from my personal brand. I strongly
ɾecommend that every person grab a hold of the concepts identified in this book.
Hajj has made the process of branding a simple one so that people can
effectively develop their brand and live their dreams."

Robert L. Johnson
Owner, NBA Charlotte Bobcats

"Flemings has offered profound insights for personal development thru the
application of brand principles. The result is an important book for anyone in or
outside of the corporate world, who seeks to grow as an individual.
A good read and time well invested."

William H. Osborne
President & Chief Executive Officer
Ford Motor Company of Canada, Ltd

'Hajj is a very bright and creative young man with an awesome vision. With his
understanding of brands and branding he has developed a successful design
firm. As he extends his reach through his latest endeavor of personal and
corporate brand management, he is an individual people will want to hear. I am
confident with his book, *The Brand YU Life* he is on the cutting edge of enabling
people, businesses and brands to
create their signature."

Robert Greenberg
Chairman, Skechers USA

"Wow, I simply love this book. I couldn't put it down once I started reading it.
Seldom does a self-help book on branding say it better than *The Brand YU Life*.
This book is a must read and see for all those who are serious about building a
brand that can compete in a very competitive market place. My heartfelt thanks
goes to Hajj Flemings for giving us this visual and well written gem."

George C. Fraser
Author, 'Click: Ten Truths for Building Extraordinary Relationships'

"I have been blessed to work with Michael Jordan and for the Jordan Brand. Through this experience, I have seen first hand one of the greatest examples of establishing a personal brand. The connection and impact branding can have on consumers spans multiple generations, athletes, businesses and cultures. Hajj has made the connection between people and brands in a way that is basic and easy to understand. The concepts of personal brand management and ideas in "The Brand YU Life" will help you redefine your life and brand values. After reading this book, I am confident that you will see the YU that you were destined to be."

D'Wayne Edwards
Director of Footwear Design
Brand Jordan (a Division of Nike)

"*The Brand YU Life* is a refreshing look at helping people develop their personal brand in order to live out their dreams. Hajj has done an excellent job of laying a solid foundation to help people understand who they are through the vehicle of personal brand management. A 'must have' in everyone's book collection."

Dr. J. Victor Eagan
Author of 'How to Discover Your Purpose in 10 Days'

"Hajj E. Flemings brand concepts equips you to reach into your soul, discover the real you and therefore unfold your true destiny."

Dr. Ben Tankard
Grammy Nominated Gospel Jazz Artist&
Senior Pastor and Founder of The Destiny Center

"*The Brand YU Life* is a wonderful introduction to the power of branding. Hajj Flemings clearly spells out why branding is so very important for everyone and provides clear frameworks and tools for building a strong personal brand."

Tim Calkins
Clinical Professor of Marketing
Kellogg School of Management, Northwestern University

The
Brand
YU Life

Re-thinking who you are
through personal brand management

Hajj E. Flemings

Third
Generation
Productions

Third
Generation
Productions

Canton, MI 48188 USA

The Brand YU Life: Re-thinking who you are through
personal brand management.

The Brand YU Life, LLC
46036 Michigan Avenue #232
Canton, MI 48188
www.hajjflemings.com
734-468-0854

Library of Congress Cataloging-in-Publication Data

Flemings, Hajj
   The Brand YU Life: Re-thinking who you are through
   personal brand management.

ISBN 0-9771388-0-1
1. Self-actualization (Psychology), 2. Creative thinking,
3. Business/Management. 4. Success — Psychological aspects.
 II. Title.   2001012345

May be purchased in bulk for educational, business, fund-raising or
sales promotional use. For information, please e-mail:
specialorders@hajjflemings.com

Broken Chains
Design Group, Inc.

Cover and Interior Design by
Broken Chains Design Group, Inc. (BCDG)
www.thebcdg.com

Published in the United States of America

table of
Contents

001°

Identify Your
Passion

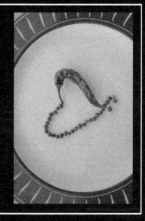

002°

Define Your
Mission

003°

Count the
Cost

table of
Contents

004°
Create Your
Voice

005°
Develop Your
Core

006°
Be
Authentic

table of
Contents

007°

Shift to
Now

Brand YU Facts

Serving Size	1 book (200 pgs)
Chapters in Book	13

Amount Per Serving

Degrees 7	**Calories from Fat 0**

% Daily Value**

Re-thinking	**100**%
who you are	
through personal	
brand management	

The Brand
YU Life

** Percent Daily Values are based on a brand
enhanced diet. Your daily values may be higher
or lower depending on your brand needs.

Change is ahead.

Change is not instant.

... you can't take a pill.

... you can't click it.

It's time to go to work.

Acknowledgments

I want to thank my wife Kasandra for her support of this book. Without her there is no me. A special thanks to all of the brands, interviewees (Hilary, D'Wayne, & Malcolm), my copy editor Elaine Israel, and countless others who contributed to this project, including my mother, from whom I get my entrepreneurial spirit. Also, I would like to acknowledge the team that helped me behind the scenes: Charles, Cynthia, and my business partner, Jomar, for their input and support.

GOLD FORMULA

For Oily Hair

O

Beautiful Hair

BRECK
SHAMPOO

15 FL. OZ.

The brand man at age 4.

Introduction

Brand YU is about branding your life. This book is about re-thinking who you are through personal brand management. Personal branding is a paradigm shift; it is a tool to help you create, define, and manage who you are. It gives you information to empower you to be the kind of person companies want to hire, the kind of person who has the skills and business acumen to take advantage of opportunities, and the kind of leader others choose to follow. Athletes, entertainers, business people and, of course, corporations and organizations large and small, have long understood the importance of branding. Now you will too.

Corporations build awareness and differentiate themselves by using brands. But branding can go beyond business to include the greatest product on the planet: Brand YU. With Brand YU, business professionals, entrepreneurs, and students can create unique personal brands and seamlessly integrate them into every aspect of their lives. Many people dream of entering the business world without realizing that they are already in business—the business of selling themselves—and that with every assignment, every project, or every job that they undertake, they are developing their resume and establishing their brand.

I developed the Brand YU message to encourage people to manage their lives with certainty and clarity. When I started to write this book, sleep went from a necessity to an interruption for me. The conclusion of this book is the start of my mission and of unlocking the door to my future. I challenge you to develop your personal brand and unlock the door to your future—much the way I had to. By reading this book, you are beginning to write your own story, create your own brand, and define your own future. You are developing the brand called YU. We live in a time where the power is being put in the hands of everyday people. Some of the most successful new businesses are based on user-generated content or peer production. Everyday people are powering successful online brands, such as MySpace, Craigslist, Amazon, Google, YouTube, and Wikipedia, to name just a few. Brand YU is about putting branding in the hands of those who don't necessarily possess marketing and branding backgrounds.

Brand YU'ers may be self-employed people or may work for others. Either way, what all successful Brand YU'ers have in common is their entrepreneurial spirit. They are smart and able to work unsupervised, a trait that will always be in demand in the business world. Entrepreneurs views themselves as self-starters who do not require external motivation to accomplish the mission at hand. Such people, those bold and passionate enough to move forward on their own, are the people who create the wealth in our society.

This book is divided into seven sections, identified as degrees. Each degree seamlessly leads to the next. I chose degrees instead of, say, rules or principles because of the significance of a degree. A degree is a small unit or interval of change. Small adjustments or units of change in re-thinking who you are can produce dramatic results in your life. The ultimate goal of the seven degrees is to eliminate the separation between you and your personal brand. The two become one entity.

My Brand Story

I grew up in a small town Roseville, Michigan with big dreams of being a footwear designer. When I was in high school, I had a passion for designing footwear. I started writing Nike during my senior year of high school and continued through my junior year of college without a positive response. In 1992, I began working for Mavade Footwear, a growing company, in Wixom, Michigan where I designed the Equator (p. 197), a cross trainer shoe. The rejection letters I received from Nike serve as an inspiration and reminder that motivate me to this day. I found that wrapped inside of every 'no' was my 'yes'. This book was birthed out of my necessity to identify my purpose and live my dreams.

Re-Thinking

The Brand
YU Life

"I now inspire others 2 live their dreams. Thx Nike-4-the inspiration."

April 29, 1991

Dear Mr. Flemings:

Thank you for your interest in the internship opportunities at our company.
We are proud of the organization and appreciate the opportunity to review
your skills and qualifications.

We are in the process of defining our internship program requirements. The
information you have provided will be reviewed for potential intern position
that become available.

Enclosed with this letter are the two designs you included with your letter
our company. It is our policy to not accept intellectual property and
inventions in this form.

Thank you again for your interest. If your background and skills match our
requirements, we will be contacting you. If you have any questions or would
like more information, please feel free to contact us.

(This letter is paraphrased for publishing.)

JUST DO IT.

PREFORTED FIRST CLASS

BEAVERTON
APR29'92
OR

U.S. POSTAGE
0.248
M METER 387661

.pril 1992

)ear Hajj,

hank you for your interest in our company's internship program, Summer
)2. Although the information you submitted was carefully reviewed, we are
onsidering other candidates who more closely match our needs.

.t our company, we value each person who includes us in their career
earch. When you have completed your studies and begin to pursue full
me employment, please contact our 24-hour job hotline. This recording
ill keep your current on available job opportunities.

.gain, thank you for making your talents known to our organization. We
ish you the best in your career search.

(This letter is paraphrased for publishing.)

Identify Your Passion

01°

Identify what you love to do. Recognizing and discovering how you are wired is key to identifying what you love to do. Identifying your passion is a fundamental principle in connecting the dots and fulfilling your mission. In the following chapters we will look at some well known brands to create a context for understanding passion as it relates to personal branding.

seven degrees° | **The Brand YU Life**

$1°$ **Identify Your Passion**

$2°$ **Define Your Mission**

$3°$ **Count the Cost**

$4°$ **Create Your Voice**

$5°$ **Develop Your Core**

$6°$ **Be Authentic**

$7°$ **Shift to Now**

C. 01

under the
influence

"Starting today you are a brand."
—*Tom Peters, author,* Re-Imagine

"It's time for me—and you—to take a lesson from the big brands, a lesson that's true for anyone who is interested in what it takes to stand out and prosper in the new world of work. Regardless of age, regardless of position, regardless of the business you are in, we all need to understand the importance of branding. We are CEOs of our own companies: Me, Inc. To be in business today, your most important job is to be head marketer for the brand called You."
—*Tom Peters, author* Re-Imagine

Branding is such an everyday part of our lives that we often don't think about it when we purchase a product—whether it's a pair of sneakers, a cup of coffee, or a mp3 player. Why shouldn't your personal brand be so readily accepted too? Brand YU is about creating a lifestyle that will help you establish your brand. Brand YU is personal branding, a fresh concept in personal brand

management (PBM). PBM is about self-discovery and bringing the real you to the surface.

What motivates you? Is it fame, power, or influence? Is it the need to feel fulfilled or to have a sense of purpose? Are you ready to define and create your life brand? Are you ready to create Brand YU? Brand YU is a requirement in our global society, which emphasizes that everything must be done in the here and now.

Brands Impact Your Life

Brands are everywhere, affecting you 24/7. Chances are that you often try unsuccessfully to avoid their influence. The use of brands in advertising and marketing is pervasive, invading every part of your life. Think of your latest movie-going experience. At the movies, where you are a captive audience, watching the film and becoming absorbed in the story, you are also viewing promotions for the latest in vehicles, fashions, appliances, soft drinks, and even cleaning products. The influence of brand marketing through movies—also known as product placement—can be powerful. Who could forget *My Big Fat Greek Wedding* and the Windex product placement? Windex was on screen seven times, for a total of 29.07 seconds. Windex sales immediately increased by almost 23 percent.

Wal-Mart's in-store television network reaches
130 million shoppers every month at the point of
decision-making. (Nielsen Media Research)

When you attend a sporting event or watch the Super Bowl, you are the recipient of a myriad of branding messages—by

24

way of commercials, songs, flashing scoreboards, and half-time shows. There is no escape. Even during the course of an ordinary day, countless impressions of brands are made on your mind. When you wander the aisles of a grocery store, your mind is bombarded with hundreds of marketing messages. This makes it difficult to clearly distinguish one product from another. With brands taking up audio, visual, and physical space it takes a clear message to cut through the interference and clutter and truly stand out in a positive manner. As a consumer you know what you look for in a brand and what features of a particular brand you find appealing. Why not put the same thought and consideration into creating your own personal brand?

During an average day, a consumer has contact with about 1,500 trademarked products.

I want to expand your thinking about the world of branding to include your personal world. Shift the paradigm of branding from product focused to people focused. Branding creates an appetite for products and services in a target audience, whether the target is a certain ethnicity, gender, age group, or even a specific economic class. No one is exempt.

Just as you are actively involved with corporate brands, you must also be actively involved with your life brand. You may not be aware of it, but you expose people, organizations, and corporations to your brand every day, sometimes in a positive way, sometimes in a negative way. So how do you become brand-minded if you've never viewed yourself as a brand? You are among the millions of people who are using technology to experiment with branding.

- Have you sold a product on eBay? (Seller)
- Have you uploaded a video to YouTube.com? (Producer)
- Have you designed a shoe at Nikeid.com? (Designer)

Average people are becoming sellers, producers, and designers every day and getting real-time experience.

The following chart identifies business and personal brands. The goal is to familiarize you with examples of personal brands. Historically we have only thought of products and services, and not people as brands.

Business Brands	vs.	Personal Brands
• Nike • Coca-Cola • MTV • Nordstroms • Tiffany & Co.	comparison	• Oprah Winfrey • Hilary Billings • Bill Gates • Steve Jobs • Michael Jordan

What attributes come to mind when you think about the business brands Nike, Coca-Cola, MTV, Nordstrom, and Tiffany & Co.? Now think about the personal brands and what attributes come to mind when you think about them.

Make Your Mark

Advertising creates discontentment, and that can be a positive force for the advertiser because the result is an opportunity to persuade a target audience that a particular product or service will satisfy them more than the one they currently use.

A brand is a promise. The challenge is turning the promise into a guarantee that its target audience will receive the real and perceived value of the product. The seller of the product banks on the loyalty that the brand fosters. In traditional business markets, a brand stands for the relationship based on trust between a company and its customers. With a successful brand, the company consistently delivers or exceeds its promised commitment to its customers.

With Brand YU, a relationship is based on you consistently delivering and exceeding job expectations or business commitments to your audience—whether it's your customers, your manager, or others with whom you interact in the course of doing business.

A brand is unique. A brand may identify one item, a family of items, or all items of one seller. Globally, more than 500,000 brands are registered with regulatory agencies. Such "official" brands are referred to as trademarks and are usually defined by the tiny TM mark that follows the name. Because a brand is unique, there is a value that is created when you are able to quantify what makes you different. The ability to capture or define what makes you stand out, makes you unique, and makes you special is crucial. Without the ability to differentiate there is no reward for being different. The trademark process is the legal system that is put in place to help organizations and companies manage the process. Developing your personal brand is the human process to help you manage your identity and the traits that differentiate you from your competition.

A brand has a reputation, yet the average person would probably be hard pressed to name 50 meaningful brands. So, how can one brand stand out? Every brand—be it from a company, religious entity, city, state, country, or individual—translates into a reputation. That reputation and what it stands for are what come to mind when a consumer deliberates about which brand to buy. Does the reputation match the true values of the brand? Do your values and character match your reputation? A shopper holding two different brands in her hands decides which to choose based partly on the reputation each has. As Naomi Klein, a leading critic of branding and author of *No Logo* states, companies are no longer selling products. Instead, "they are selling brands that evoke a subtle mix of people's hopes, dreams, and aspirations." As a personal brand you are not just selling your skills and abilities, you are meeting expectations, hopes, and emotional needs of people and customers.

**As a personal brand you must consistently
deliver on your promises. Your employer or your
clients must be able to depend on you to perform tasks
completely, thoroughly, and with high-level results.**

There Are No Accidents

Successful branding does not happen by accident. Top marketers leave little to chance when they send their message to you. They invest millions of dollars to expose consumers to their brands. Over time, the consumer comes to learn and understand what benefits a brand offers. Imagine life without brands. Imagine eating breakfast flakes and not seeing an icon like Tony the Tiger on the box. Imagine dressing in label-free clothes. Would you think of driving an unbranded car or turning on your TV without knowing which branded stations are which? Your entire decision-making process about how to spend your money and time would change.

**People will pay more for a product or
service that consistently delivers on
its promises.**

You are under the influence of brands with almost every decision that you make. Brands simplify choices, reduce risk for the consumer, and allow consumers to make decisions with confidence. Brands are shortcuts in the decision-making process. Without its brand, a product is just a commodity. For example, people rarely purchase vehicles based purely upon specifications (for example, engine type, vehicle weight, horsepower, and fuel economy). Although buyers do consider their needs and conduct research to determine which vehicles might best meet those needs, in the end, they will be influenced by the brand marketing messages that the various vehicles represent.

**"A genuine brand makes a promise and delivers
on that promise in a distinctive way."**
—*Duane E. Knapp, president of BrandStrategy*

You Are Not a Commodity

Just as branding helps to differentiate a product or service from the competition, personal branding enhances and packages your abilities and increases your market value. Without a personal brand, you are simply a commodity. Without a personal brand marketing message, people cannot know whether or not you can meet their needs. By the way, branding is fun! Have fun learning how to stand out. Having the skills and talent to do a job well is not enough to succeed. As the U.S. economy takes a major turn, American corporations are being pressured to stay increasingly more competitive, so they outsource jobs to other countries. If your job can be done cheaper somewhere else, it is a candidate to be outsourced. You have to re-think your life and work. Brand building is a requirement in the new economy. When you were a child, it was probably assumed that you would go to school, start a career, and work in your chosen field until death. In the new economy the expectation that anyone will work for 30 to 40 years at one job or in the same field no longer exists. The only dynamic that remains the same is change. The need for individuals—including you—to be better and smarter and to distinguish who they are is of increasing importance.

Suppose a buyer is choosing between three vehicles: Vehicle X, Vehicle Y, and Vehicle Z, and that only X and Y have strong brand marketing messages; therefore, Z will be perceived as a commodity, which a buyer will not consider because he or she will believe there is no way to know if the product will meet his or her needs.

Great Brands

"[Branding] . . . makes you want to put Nike on your feet, Disney in your vacation, and Häagen-Dazs in your refrigerator."
—*David A. Shore, Associate Director, Trust Initiatives, School of Public Health, Harvard University*

Nike . . . Starbucks . . . Tiffany & Co. . . . BMW . . . Apple . . . Dell . . . Harley-Davidson

Do you know what qualities make these brands great? Some key elements are mission statements, brand identity, and packaging. The same characteristics apply regardless of the size of the organization or company. The brand is the intangible asset of an organization. An excellent case in point is the car maker Bentley. When Bentley's assets were liquidated, its manufacturing facilities, tooling, and equipment were sold for $20 million. The brand, the logo, and name—the intangible assets of the company—were sold to BMW for an additional $20 million.

As you begin to consider the importance of personal branding, consider the following questions.

- What is your brand worth?
- Are you building equity?
- What are your intangible assets?

Your financial health, values, routine, resources, vision, and mission statement (your purpose) are the basic critical components of your brand. A brand has "arrived" when it is perceived by the target audience as the only solution to a need. Thus, when you are marketing your personal brand to a target audience, say a potential employer, a volunteer committee, or your co-workers, it's essential to have a clearly identifiable brand that will be perceived as the ideal solution to your audience's needs. Your name, your reputation, your talent, your knowledge, and your skills are all marketable assets. But true personal branding requires discipline, transparency, and authenticity to make it work. You must be totally committed to developing your life brand if you expect it to succeed. You need to incorporate and consistently practice the application of branding. This is an easy task for some people, but for others it is a difficult challenge. Remember: brands are based upon trust. The trust of customers is the foundation of every successful brand. As you develop your personal brand, you must begin with trusting yourself. You must be prepared to overcome feelings of doubt, insecurity, creative barriers, and psychological obstacles to create your future.

The Raw Ingredients

If you analyze some of the top brands and their main products, you'll realize how basic their raw ingredients are. For example, without coffee beans at Starbucks, there is no caffeine beckoning the millions of customers. At the heart of every successful brand is the raw material for which the brand is known. And, as the following chart illustrates, the raw ingredients may not be costly or rare. Nevertheless, the customer values the product. The product's ingredients may even induce an emotional attachment, leading consumers to eventually purchase the product because of that attachment rather than because the product fills a genuine need.

Brand	Raw Ingredients
Coca-Cola	caramel + water
Starbucks	coffee beans + water
McDonald's	meat (hamburgers) + potatoes (fries)

- Coca-Cola (established 1886) is a carbonated beverage and has a brand value of $67.5 billion.
- Starbucks (established 1971) sells coffee and has a brand value of $2.5 billion.
- McDonald's (established 1954) was built on hamburgers and french fries and has a brand value of $26 billion.
  (Source: *BusinessWeek*, "2005 Top 100 Brands")

Great brands are built on a good idea that depends on basic elements. Thus, the success of Coca-Cola, Starbucks, and McDonald's is based upon the differentiation of their brand elements. Similar to a successfully branded product, you are a combination of your raw elements. These need to be harnessed to create the power required to propel your brand to the next level. Your skills, talents, and abilities are qualities with unlimited potential. Stop and think about your raw ingredients. How can you package what you already have and produce a powerful result?

Now look at yourself as a collection of raw materials that have been processed, packaged, and presented to your customer as a brand. Personal branding helps you to create the experience that is expected by your audience, which may include the management of your company, your supervisor, and clients.

Every successful brand has:

- **Name Recognition:** The product name is recognized by the target market.
- **Brand Image:** The way in which the product is perceived by the target audience.
- **Brand Position:** The need the product is perceived as meeting.
- **Brand Promise:** What the brand's marketing message promises the product will do.

What impact do these elements have on a personal brand? Think Michael Jordan. Think Jack Welch. Think Martha Stewart. They have name recognition. They have an image of excellence. Personal branding (and some talent and charisma, too, of course) allows Michael Jordan to charge grown men $15,000 to attend the week-long Michael Jordan Senior Flight Basketball Camp. It allows Jack Welch, the former CEO of GE, to earn $9.2 million on the lecture circuit and helped him become the top earning public speaker of 2004, according to *Forbes* magazine. Even after Martha Stewart's incarceration, her image still tested well with her target market. Michael, Jack, and Martha deliver on their promises. Michael Jordan's six championship rings allow him to present himself as someone who can lead with authority. Similarly, after attending a Jack Welch speech, his listeners feel empowered and believe that they too can accomplish what Jack accomplished. Martha shows her audience how just about anyone can have a beautiful home and make wonderful meals on a budget. These market leaders are positioned as experts in their fields. They can make their audiences walk away feeling as if they, too, can become experts.

Creative Brand Advertising

In today's markets, companies are becoming increasingly creative in communicating their brand message. Branding abhors a vacuum. Is there public space available? Use it to create branding. You now see brands placed in creative ways everywhere you look. Nike and Apple, for example, are two companies that use public space to increase brand awareness. In 2004, Apple transformed the St. George subway station in downtown Toronto by branding the posts, walls, stairs, and newspaper recycle bins with iPod marketing. Nike has gone even further in its branding of public space. The sneaker company started the revolutionary Nike Ground campaign. Nike is introducing its legendary brand into squares, streets, parks, and boulevards: Nikesquare, Nikestreet, Piazzanike,

Plazanike, or Nikestrasse will appear in major world capitals over the coming years. In Austria, Karlsplatz, one of Vienna's beautiful and historic squares, has been renamed Nikeplatz. The tagline for the marketing campaign is "You want to wear it, why shouldn't cities wear it too?" Nike is forcing cities to rethink space. How far will Nike go with its branding efforts? How far will you go with your branding efforts? The answer for both should be the same: As far as it will be allowed. Just like corporations, you, too, can use nontraditional ways to distinguish yourself from the masses. The expansion of technology and the Internet have resulted in unique ways to do that. It is time to think outside the corrugated box and open your mind to new definitions of workspace, environment, career, and life planning.

Overcoming Obstacles

What keeps you from attempting the seemingly impossible? You are often your greatest obstacle. Mental barriers and fear are self-imposed forces that can be minimized and overcome, even eliminated. Your experience has been woven in the fabric of your life brand.

Your Evolving Brand

The beautiful part of brands is that they evolve with time. Seamlessly integrating branding into your life will allow you to systematically and effectively manage your brand. You will feel your brand's impact in a variety of ways, depending on your goals. Life has taught you many business lessons, the kind people pay a great deal of money to learn from educators, business coaches, or consultants, and the kind you learn from personal experience. Can you apply what you have learned? Plan your work and work your plan. Do you know where the next great idea lies? It probably lies dormant within you, like a bear in hibernation. But now is the time to awaken the idea. It's time to nourish your vision so it will flourish.

Daily Download

Exercise #1a: Identify your three favorite brands.

_____

_____

_____

Exercise #1b: What need does each of these brands promise to fulfill?

1. _____

2. _____

3. _____

"Gary Erickson's Clif Bar ascended from a homemade energy bar to a $100 million phenomenon with an estimated 35 million customers and a company hailed by *Inc.* magazine as one of the fastest-growing private companies in the United States four years in a row."

www.clifbar.com

John Winter Smith, a software developer from Houston, Texas, spent $10,000 over seven years trying to visit every Starbucks in the world. He has visited—and had a vente cup of coffee—at 4,300 stores worldwide.

C. 02
pure passion

"There will always be a premium
for people who are better than others."
—*Matthew Budman, author,*
   Instant Expert: Collecting Books

Your life is based on movement, on advancing toward
your vision. It involves a series of steps moving you
toward re-thinking and redefining your life. Passion is a
force; brands move us emotionally and compel us to
want the perceived value and the lifestyle that we associate with them. Brands carry with them a feeling of significance. When you hear the names Tiffany & Co., Ritz-
Carlton, Maybach, and Gucci, what comes to mind?
Think about the following two words:

Significance

Existence

Living a life of significance is fueled by passion.
Passionless people exist. Passionate people create the
future. Brands can take on a life of their own. Some

brands invoke a passion in us that we may not even be aware of. Most people are not very passionate about brands that don't give that feeling of significance.

In my research to develop this book I felt that Karl D. Speak and David McNally, co-authors of *Be Your Own Brand,* best defined brand and personal brand management (PBM) as follows.

Brand
A brand is a perception or emotion, maintained by a buyer or prospective buyer, describing the experience related to doing business with an organization or consuming its products and services.

Personal Brand Management
Your brand is a perception or emotion, maintained by some-body other than you, that describes the total experience of having a relationship with you.

The context of PBM is driven by three key elements that help bring clarity and significance: Relevance, Uncommonness, and Relentlessness.

- **Relevance**. Your mission, which is your purpose, must be relevant.The passion that is on the inside of you was created to be relevant. You were born during the greatest time in human history, with something special to contribute to the world. But being relevant — pertinent, applicable, and significant — directly connects with who you are and has as much to do with context as it does time. What you have to offer has to be what people are willing to pay or appropriately expect.

The top selling laundry detergent in America is Tide, which was created to clean clothes. If its mission changes and the product specifications are held constant, the product could become ineffective. For example, if you take Tropic Clean Tide and attempt to use it as a soft drink, this would be an inappropriate application of this brand, making it ineffective. It is only revelant within its proper context.

- **Uncommonness.** This means being distinctive, standing out, marked as different, prominent, rare, exceptional, remarkable, above the ordinary, not an ordinary encounter. Quit being extremely ordinary and become *extra* ordinary. Be different. Stand out in a remarkable way when people encounter or interact with you.

- **Relentlessness.** You must be unyielding in your pursuit of excellence. In pursuing your passion, be willing to give everything that you have and to not leave anything to chance.

People who passionately pursue the desire that gives them significance possess these three qualities. Passion is an intense, driving, or overmastering feeling or conviction about an object of desire or deep interest in something. We are all passionate about something: the pursuit becomes recognition of that passion. In the same way that you have intense feelings about your favorite brands, you should have an intense passion about your vocation. Unfortunately, passion and work are rarely used in the same sentence. This is an important point to keep in mind as you develop your personal brand and identify the vocation that defines you and that you feel passionate about. Your future, your greatness is tied to your personal passion. The emotional connection, the passion, the drive that you have to do the thing that makes you unique is passion. The thing that makes you stand out is passion. It is hard-wired into your DNA, it is coded on the inside of you. It is the fire that burns deep within. Most of us ignore the drive, and focus instead on what other people have told us we ought to be, or on what we see others do. However, it is difficult to be great at something that you were never created to do.

Your passion should inspire you. Identifying your passion will help you to direct your energy and unlock your skills, ideas, and abilities to perform specific tasks that give you fulfillment. Each of us feels passionate about something. Identifying your passion is the key to a great Brand YU.

Personal branding is about setting yourself apart from the competition. A brand that you purchase can make you feel different, but won't necessarily change you. On the other hand, what you feel passionate about, your personal brand, may change and inspire every aspect of your life.

The Emotional Connection of Brands

Compare each of the personal and product brands in the table on the following page and see the emotional thread that connects both. As the table shows, personal branding is based on similar principles as product branding; a key difference, however, is that the motivation and reward for personal branding are intrinsic rather than extrinsic.

Brand YU	vs.	Commerical Brands
• Being paid for what I love to do		• Paying for brands that I love
• Something that I must achieve	comparison	• Something that I must have
• I would pursue my passion without being motivated by money		• I want this regardless of the price
• I feel good when I am doing a certain task		• I feel good when I have this particular item
• My passion strongly influences my lifestyle		• Brands I like are a part of the lifestyle that I desire

Identifying Your Passion

- Natural Abilities: What gifts and talents do you have?
- Interests: What do you like to do?
- Exposure: What opportunities have you had access to?

Why are a lot of people unhappy with their life? It is because they are living someone else's life, doing something that they were never created to do. The work skills that they are using are incompatible with their talent and natural abilities.

The Passion Principle ...
- . . . inspires action.
- . . . resonates with your mission.
- . . . energizes you and your environment.

This principle is based on a journey. This journey takes time; recognizing and pursuing your passion is not a short-term commitment. My job is to help you embark on that journey, to recognize the passion within you, and to teach you how to tap into it that passion and bring it to the surface. For example, suppose someone approached me and said they would pay me $1 million a year if I committed to go fishing 12 hours a day, six days a week for the next 30 years, with a balloon payment of $5 million at the end of the last year. I am not a fisherman by trade nor for a hobby, but I could physically meet the commitment. My passion for fishing, however, would not increase because of the money. There is no need to chase money if you understand that it follows the passion and does not create it. It would be difficult for me to sustain an interest in fishing, not because I am not a hard worker, but because fishing is neither my vocation nor my passion. In much the same way, the Brand YU person has developed an understanding of the importance of choosing the occupation to which he or she can be truly committed. Such a person understands that money doesn't create passion.The purpose of having passion should be to propel you to move to the next step: the development of your mission.

Daily Download

Exercise #2: List three things you would do without money as the motivation.

1. _____

2. _____

3. _____

"The starting point of all achievement is desire. Keep this constantly in mind. Weak desires bring weak results, just as a small amount of fire makes a small amount of heat."

—*Napoleon Hill, author,* Think and Grow Rich

Identify what you are meant to accomplish. Passionately define your purpose, the reason for your existence. Each person was designed to accomplish something specific. We are creatively designed and equipped to accomplish our mission through conversion, — conversion of vision, text, and audio. In this chapter we will discuss the role of being equipped with the right tools to enable you to accomplish your purpose.

02°

Baggage Claim
Ticketing/Check-in
ATS
Terminals 1 2 3 5

"Singleness of purpose is one of the chief essentials for success in life, no matter what may be one's aim."

—John D. Rockefeller, American industrialist

The vision & mission minded person

"When you discover your mission, you will feel its demand. It will fill you with enthusiasm and a burning desire to get to work on it."
—*W. Clement Stone, co-author,*
Success Through a Positive Mental Attitude

Your mission should be one of self-discovery, of becoming the person you were meant to be, the person with ideas, potential, energy, and a destiny that cannot be contained. You were meant to pass by small thinkers, "crybabies," complainers, and individuals who use excuses to cover inefficiency and feelings of insecurity. Your life is your property. It's time to stop renting and start owning. To achieve success you need a vision of where you are heading. Be clear about your vision and always keep it before you. Hang it on the wall. Put it in your PDA. Save it as a voice memo in your iPod.

"**Business enterprises— and public service institutions— are organs of society. They do not exist for their own sake, but to fulfill a specific social purpose and to satisfy a specific need of a society, a community, or individuals. They are not ends in themselves, but means.**"

—*Peter Drucker, author,* The Daily Drucker

Visionary Thinking

Having a vision has little to do with what you can actually see. Seeing what is tangible doesn't necessarily mean you have vision, it just means you have sight. In fact, sight is affected by the other four senses and can be a barrier to vision. Vision is about recognizing the intangible and making it real.

Just about every successful brand originated with a visionary man or woman whose imagination, presence, courage, and passion were vital to the growth and success of the brand. Are such individuals unusual? Are they born with an innate ability? No. Vision can be developed.

A visionary sees a desired future and develops a strategy to bring it into sight. One way this is accomplished is through visualization. Visualization is defined as the formation of mental visual images.

Visualization is a tool that athletes and highly successful people use. Your mind is a powerful instrument that is capable of helping you process information to produce greater results. When your mind creates an image on the inside, it cannot tell the difference between the real thing and the image. This is the reason that visualization is so powerful: The picture that you see on the inside becomes your reality and you then begin to act on it.

Examples:

- Tiger Woods visualizes putting the ball in the cup every time he steps on the green.
- Michael Jordan visualized taking last second shots to win games.

The power of visualization is an awesome tool. It is your internal video camera. It is time to develop positive audio and video content that is internally generated. Everyone is created with the ability to create images on the inside. As you begin to think about your mission and where you see yourself, a picture is being downloaded internally. Listed below are the three steps of mission statement development. They are:

1. Downloading the image inside
2. Converting the image into text (mission statement, or written word)
3. Converting the text to audio (spoken word)

Passion is the fire that ignites the vision. A fire can be sustained when there is an adequate and continuous supply of oxygen. To keep the fire burning or the passion alive you have to speak the vision. Otherwise, your vision, your passion, will suffocate and die. When is the last time that you saw yourself as successful? It is time to start visualizing your success.

Visionaries visualize, visionaries "see things," they even talk to themselves. Other people sometimes think they are a little off, until the vision becomes reality. The visionaries then become "eccentric," "a great mind," and "brilliant." A visionary sees further, sees more, sees before others and is willing to do the work needed to cause the vision to materialize. Although we are not all born visionaries, we all have the tools and skills we need to develop visionary thinking in ourselves.

A visionary starts with a mission—and so should you. Everybody has a mission; however, in many cases it is underdeveloped, leading people to pursue the developed mission of someone else. It is easier to chase after someone else's vision because it requires less work and accountability, but is also yields less results. Truly mission-minded people use their vision to make informed short-term decisions and to plan long-term direction and strategy for themselves.

Recognizing Your Mission

What wakes you up in the morning? I'm not referring to your alarm clock or the caffeine in your latte. Instead, I'm referring to a driving force that cannot be seen, heard, or tasted. Your goal, you mission, your purpose is what gives you that jolt in the morning. As Viktor E. Frankl, the Austrian psychologist, said, "Everyone has his own specific vocation or mission in life; everyone must carry out a concrete assignment that demands fulfillment. Therein he cannot be replaced, nor can his life be repeated." The missions of most companies and organizations are embodied in a mission statement that states what the organization is, what products or services it produces or provides, what market(s) it serves, and what its goals are. Imagine how perfect it would be to work in an environment with people whose personal missions are aligned with those of their organizations. Think about what a successful company with such an environment would produce!

> **"With respect to . . . business purpose and business mission, there is only one focus. . . . It is the customer. The customer defines the business. A business is not defined by the company's name, status, or articles of incorporation. It is defined by the want a customer satisfies when he or she buys a product or a service. To satisfy the customer is the mission and purpose of every business. The question "What is our business?" can, therefore, be answered only by looking at the business . . . from the point of view of customer and market. All the customer is interested in are his or her own values, wants, and reality."**
>
> *—Peter Drucker, author,* The Daily Drucker

Look at the similarities of mission statements between business brands and personal brands. As you can see in the following chart, a personal mission statement addresses many of the areas that a corporate mission statement does, but uses different terminology.

Business Brands	**vs.**	**Personal Brands**
• Corporate culture • Target customers • Products & services • Strategic planning	comparison	• Personal values • Audience/clients • Skills/abilities • Measurable goals

Corporate Brand Mission Statements

Ford Motor Company
"To become the world's leading consumer company for automotive products and services."

Google
"Organize the world's information and make it universally accessible and useful."

Dell Computers
"To be the most successful computer company in the world at delivering the best customer experience in markets we serve."

Coca-Cola
"To put a can of Coke within arms reach of everyone on the planet."

Häagen-Dazs
"To provide every customer with the highest quality dessert-eating experience."

Starbucks
"Establish Starbucks as the premier purveyor of the finest coffee in the world while maintaining our uncompromising principles while we grow."

The Oprah Winfrey Show
"To use television to transform people's lives, to make viewers see themselves differently, and to bring happiness and a sense of fulfillment into every home."

American Red Cross

To be "a humanitarian organization led by volunteers and guided by its Congressional Charter and the fundamental principles of the International Red Cross Movement, will provide relief to victims of disasters and help people prevent, prepare for, and respond to emergencies."

Some brands, such as Mary Kay and Harvard University, are iconic; they immediately come to mind when we think of the products they represent because they have established themselves as the standard for their industry. Here are Mary Kay's and Harvard's mission statements.

Mary Kay

"To give unlimited opportunity to women."

Harvard University

"To strive to create knowledge, to open the minds of students to that knowledge, and to enable students to take the best advantage of their educational opportunities."

Like successful corporations, those who want to be successful in their professional and personal lives must also have a mission— a purpose that guides them in their daily lives. Here is my own mission statement.

Personal Mission Statement

Hajj E. Flemings, Brand Strategist

"To be a voice that inspires, drives, and compels others to greatness, enabling people, businesses, and brands to create their signature."

Developing Your Mission Statement

To create your vision and make it a reality, you must download the image on the inside and convert it to text, or plainly put, put it in writing. You will have the opportunity to do this at the end of this chapter. Your Brand YU mission statement is your life statement. It should guide your activities, lifestyle, and decisions. A mission statement is a living document that changes as the demands of your life change. But the statement is more than just words on paper. You, the brand, the individual, make your mission statement come alive. And by adhering to your personal mission, as expressed in your mission statement, you will distinguish yourself as one whom others seek out. Your mission statement should define and even improve your world. Your mission statement needs to be about your life and your goals.

To understand your mission, ask:

- Is my life making a statement? What is that statement?

- Does it arouse interest in others?

- Can it challenge me, draw people to me, and position me to capitalize on opportunities for personal advancement?

Your mission statement must recognize what makes you unique. Other people and businesses make decisions about dealing with you based upon their perception of you. Your reputation and your actions help to shape that impression and reflect the opinion that people have of you. As a successful brand, you are in the people business; therefore, managing relationships is critical to your personal success.

As you contemplate your personal mission statement, you must clearly articulate your vision to yourself, so that you can then commit your idea to paper. Play the vision over and over in your head. Write it in a clear and concise format that is easy to understand and provides you with clear direction and insight. As you begin to write your statement, it may seem difficult to define your mission. But as you better understand the skills and abilities you have to offer, you will be able to more clearly state them.

Think about yourself as a well-designed product. Developing an effective mission statement will help you sort out business opportunities. As your influence and power increase, you will find more and more opportunities will be open to you. You will have to effectively select the opportunities that best help you fulfill your personal mission. If you keep your mission in mind as you review business opportunities, you will know whether an opportunity is a good fit or not.

America's best-known visionaries, such as Henry Ford, John D. Rockefeller, Bill Gates, and Steve Jobs, understood that they had a special assignment. That assignment consumed them, and drove them to the tireless development of their ideas. Although you may have a good idea of what you want to do and accomplish in life, the next step is to focus on understanding and defining your mission.

Keys to Your Mission Statement

1) **Recognize your style.** Identify what makes you unique.

2) **Identify your fit.** Realistically define your future.

3) **Live your mission with pride.** Your statement represents you and your mission, so be proud to identify with it and to have it represent your values and aspirations. Acquiring an outsized vision can frustrate you instead of stretching you.

4) **Be concise (15 to 25 words).**

5) Make your statement easy to understand.

6) Make it meaningful to you.

Your mission statement should be long enough to communicate your purpose, but short enough to focus on the key message. It should be straightforward so that it can be understood by anyone reading it. And when you read it, it should resonate with you.

A mission statement isn't static. It must be updated to reflect your changing circumstances. However, it should be updated only when it has outlived its current status. Microsoft, for example, updated its mission statement from a "PC in every home" to "empowering people through great software—any time, any place, and on any device," once the company felt it had achieved its original mission statement.

Tools for Your Mission

After you have identified your mission, the next step is defining the tools for the mission. In the hands of the right person, a tool has greater value than the price paid to acquire it. For example, a Nike five iron in Tiger Woods' hands has helped him earn more than $200 million. A leather Spaulding basketball in the hands of Michael Jordan has resulted in an economic impact of $10 billion. Connect your natural abilities to the tools/equipment that are required for your purpose. Every professional has tools that he or she must utilize and develop. What are your tools?

Every successful person has a story, and history will remember the person because of what he or she accomplished. Regardless of what else Tiger does in life, he will always be a golfer. Regardless of what else Oprah does, she will always be a talk show host.

Recognition of what distinguishes you is key in identifying the tools for your mission. How will history remember you? How will you be known?

 Daily Download

Exercise #3: Create your mission statement
(in 25 words or less).

_____

_____

_____

_____

_____

"I knew early on that the news business was right for me. I enjoyed it, it was fun. If I thought it was work, I might not have done it."

—*Sam Donaldson, ABC News Correspondent*

s m l XL 2X

"In the modern world, it is useless
to be a creative, original thinker unless
you are able to sell what you create."
    —*David Ogilvy, Legendary Advertising Executive*

What are you? Free agent. Employee.
Temp worker. Freelancer. Salary
Worker. Knowledge worker.   Artist.
Unemployed. Entrepreneur. Student.
Intrapreneur.   Stay-at-home mother.
Self-employed.   Mogul.   Investor.
Professional Student.   Comedian.
Consultant. Actor. Musician. Model.
Displaced Worker.   Salesperson.
Athlete.   Blogger.   Webpreneur.
Politician.

Ask anyone what they want to be and you will get an idea of their mission. What were you created to do? Apple trees are planted to produce apples. Ford Motor Company was created to produce cars. Coca-Cola was created to produce soda/pop/Coke (depends on where you live). Nike was created to produce athletic products/sneakers. But these brands were created to produce more than just a product, they were created to produce an experience. Over time each one of these brands has expanded in its geographic footprint and product offerings, much the same way a person relocates, changes careers, and shifts from working for someone to working for themselves. You were created to produce high-level work. Your success is directly linked to you operating in your lane. A person who operates in his or her purpose can tap into creativity at a deeper level. A person who operates in his or her purpose must think outside the box.

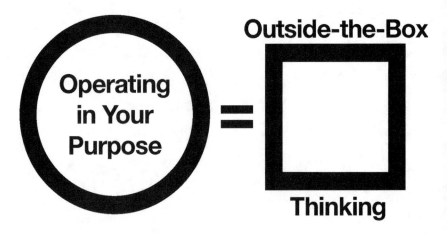

Do the rich and famous have all the fun? No, it is those who understand their life purpose who get the most out of life. Working in your purpose increases your worth. Instead of watching the clock, counting down the hours until you can go home, you enjoy working because you are in your purpose.

When you enjoy your work, you become creative. Your creativity can turn a mistake into a multi-million dollar idea. Consider these examples.

- **Post-it-notes:** The original adhesive used in Post-it notes was invented in 1968 by Spencer Silver, a 3M researcher. While attempting to design a strong adhesive, he instead developed an adhesive that was very weak. No immediate application was apparent. In 1974, one of Silver's colleagues, Arthur Fry, was frustrated because the notes from his hymn book kept falling out. This gave him the idea to create the Post-it-notes. Initial prototypes were available in 1977, and by 1980–81, after a large sampling campaign, the product had been introduced around the world, being produced exclusively in Cynthiana, Kentucky.

- **Play-Doh:** This product was invented by Noah and Joseph McVicker in 1956. One of many common products invented by accident, it was meant as a wallpaper cleaner. Joe McVicker became a millionaire before his twenty-seventh birthday after re-releasing the product as a toy.

- **Potato chips:** In the summer of 1853, Native American George Crum was employed as a chef at an elegant resort in Saratoga Springs, New York. One dinner guest found Crum's french fries too thick for his liking and rejected the order. Crum decided to rile the guest by producing fries too thin and crisp to skewer with a fork. The plan backfired. The guest was ecstatic over the browned, paper-thin potatoes, and other diners began requesting Crum's potato chips.

Branding is expanding into public spaces, new markets, and

new products. Personal branding is about growth and development. For successful personal branding, you must expand your vision, expand your voice, expand your reach, expand your influence, and expand your brand. New technology, resources, and markets come at a price. Expansion of your brand will cost, but anything of value usually does.

Brand YU Categories

The principles to extend your brand are the same, but the development path you pursue is based upon your work situation. Some people prefer to work for others, while others like the challenge of running a business. In both groups are courageous and visionary souls whose drive empowers them to define industries and create essential brands. When it comes to their life's work, members of all the groups are "preneurs"—either entrepreneurs or intrapreneurs.

- **Entrepreneur:** One who organizes, manages, and assumes the risks of a business or enterprise, and pursues opportunity without regard to resources currently controlled.

- **Intrapreneur:** One who applies entrepreneurial skills within an established corporation or organization.

The following categories represent three levels of career and professional achievement. Read each description carefully to understand which category best aligns with your work life plans, and best describes you and identifies your desired future state.

1. Builders (Employees)

2. Leapers (Self-employed)

   2.5. Extreme Leapers (Self-employed & Influential)

3. Zoomers (Highly successful builders or leapers)

Builders

A Builder is one who works for an established or existing corporation or organization. A Builder is an intrapreneur and is likely to be:

- Employed by an organization or company where he or she is expected to produce high-level work.

- A mission-minded person who works in his or her chosen field as an employee.

- An individual who prefers the security and structure of working for an established corporation or organization.

- Focused on job assignments versus the viability of the organization (exceptions are those at the top of senior management).

- Averse to the risk of self-employment.

(Examples: Jack Welch, General Electric; Lee Iacocca, Chrysler; Carl Levin, Michigan Senator)

Leapers

A Leaper is one who springs free from the Builder state (from working as an employee). He or she assumes the risk of managing a business as self-employed or as an employer. A Leaper is an entrepreneur and is likely to be:

- An individual who organizes, manages, and assumes the risks of a business or enterprise.

- Self-employed, a freelancer, or an independent contractor.

- An employer, owner/founder of a company, or franchisee.

- A professional (model, entertainer, and athlete).

- An individual whose personality, skills, style, and abilities are leveraged to build or promote a brand.

(Examples: Veronica Webb, model; Dave Bing, Bing Steel)

Extreme Leapers: This category is that of high achieving Leapers. Most people aren't willing to put in the time or have not developed themselves to a high enough level to achieve the Extreme Leaper status. Extreme Leapers are likely to be:

- Individuals who have led the day-to-day functions of an organization or corporation and have built the brand that is widely recognized within their industry.

- Individuals who started on a journey to pursue their passion and found themselves creating an entity that was bigger than they were. Extreme Leapers believe they have a higher calling to make a valuable contribution to the world.

- Those who have achieved substantial success and are looking for the next plateau.

- Individuals with the ability, vision, and passion to develop businesses or an organization whose ideas, products, and services stand the test of time.

- Extremely motivated and passionate.

- Innovative and motivated to get their ideas, thoughts, andproducts to the world.

- Their main or core business and source of financial income is generated in this category.

(Example: Henry Ford, Ford Motor Company and Malcolm Alexander, Alexander Global Promotions)

Zoomers

Zoomers have a mastery of purpose that propels them to high net worth and influence. A Zoomer is an entrepreneur and is likely to:

- Have elite status.

- Have a high net worth developed through operating in his or her purpose.

- Possess mastery of purpose.

- Have name recognition outside of his or her industry.

- Be self-employed or the founder of a company or an organization. It is more difficult to go this level as an employee.

- Operating multiple businesses and multiple income streams.

(Examples: Bill Gates, Microsoft; Steve Jobs, Apple; and Oprah Winfrey, Oprah Show)

Some people build, some people leap, but everyone wants to zoom. As I conducted research on personal brands there are the classic examples of each type that I had to use to effectively communicate the point. These were also people whom you could relate to that easily showed the point. What I thought would be interesting was to use brand leaders who affect our everyday life but who most people have never heard of. I wanted to use real people. Each one of these individuals has impacted my life directly or indirectly.

In this chapter we will look at D'Wayne Edwards, a designer for Brand Jordan. This takes me back to 1984 when I got my first pair of Air Jordan gymshoes, which cost $65. At the time my team uniform was Carolina blue and white. My gym shoes were red/black/white, but I didn't care. D'Wayne Edwards fueled my passion for footwear design when we worked together at Mavade Footwear. I was a college intern and he was a seasoned designer. A second case study is Hilary Billings. After graduating from college and purchasing my first home, I remember going to Pottery Barn and the sense of modern comfort that I felt when I walked into the store. I just wanted to buy something. I made my first Pottery Barn purchase, at a cost of about $15. It was a stainless steel candle holder.

Builders are around us every day; they are the men and women who are employed at corporations, organizations, churches, and institutions of higher learning, making the world a better place. When I think of Builders, Jack Welch and Lee Iacocca come to mind. Two of the greatest CEOs of modern history. Builders are individuals who enjoy working for established businesses. Builders build a better tomorrow, with the tools that are created and in place today. Terms used to describe this category of workers include: *employees and knowledge workers.*

Case Study
Hilary Billings
Category: Builder

Look around your home. Are there unique pieces that give your home its special feeling of "hominess"? Are there pieces that make you feel different when you step inside your home? If so, Hilary Billings may be one of the reasons. Hilary Billings, an Art-History/English Literature double major from Brown University, is the major force behind the turn around to make Pottery Barn, the purveyor of fashionable, high-quality home furnishings, a household name.

Hilary's first emotional connection with the power of branding came when she was a teenager, before she even realized what a brand was. Her father loved to cook and loved Williams-Sonoma (coincidentally, the parent company of Pottery Barn). Most men go to a store for function only, but not her father. Hilary recalls that her father went to Williams-Sonoma because of the way he felt when he was there. That emotional connection to the joy of gourmet cooking, that promise that he would feel a certain way when he walked in the store, is Hilary's definition of branding.

After graduating from Brown University, Hilary was on her way to pursuing her graduate degree when her father encouraged her to get out and experience life. So, instead of graduate school, Hilary participated in the executive program at Macy's. There she realized she had an eye for detail that could be used to her advantage on a larger scale. In 1991, she started as a buyer for Pottery Barn's catalogue division. One year later, Hilary became the director of the Pottery Barn Catalogue and did something shocking. She put a sofa on the cover of the catalogue—before Pottery Barn even had one in the store! This move revolutionized the home catalogue business and was one of the bold moves that revived Pottery Barn's business.

After seven years with Pottery Barn, Hilary decided it was time for a new challenge. She took her theme of lifestyle brands to the Starwood Hotels & Resorts, now the parent company of the Sheraton & Westin Hotels. There was definitely a hole in the business hotel industry for a hotel that embraced individually, style, and the comfort of home. Hilary welcomed the challenge of filling that gap and transformed Starwood's W Hotel into the hotel of choice for the business traveler. In 1999, she took the theme of lifestyle brands in yet another direction with RedEnvelope, Inc., an Internet company that specializes in upscale business and personal gifts.

When asked what separates her in the field of branding, Hilary Billings says, "I am very focused on what inspires people emotionally. When someone makes an emotional connection, people often think it is just about the heart. Actually, it's about the brain and the science behind it. It's the unspoken scientific, intellectual side of branding that keeps unconscientiously coming back." Hilary Billings, an Independent Brand Strategist, loves her life. She has four sons, does two days of consulting each week and often works from home. When asked the secret of her success, Hilary reflects, "People are connected to their passion, but often put it aside to pursue a career. Their careers are often about a big job, a big title, big spending, but doing little of what they love. At the end, you realize the 'big' things were not enough. Connect with smaller companies, give projects your full attention and detail. You can build organically and become 'big' over time. Believe me, it's worth the energy and time."

Case Study
D'Wayne Edwards
Category: Builder

Today, D'Wayne Edwards is the Design Director for Brand Jordan footwear and is living his dream. He has designed over 40 different styles for Nike, in their ACG (All-Condition Gear), L.E. Active Life, and Jordan brands. His path to footwear greatness has been a winding road that has challenged his resolve and caused him to question his desire to pursue his lifelong dream.

The beginning of Edwards' journey is not an uncommon one. He is one of six children raised in Inglewood, California, by a single mother. Money was a scarce resource in D'Wayne's family and the idea of a career as a footwear designer was foreign to him. At the age of 12, he designed his first shoe with no idea that he was nurturing a passion that would unlock his future. As he entered high school, he looked for direction on how to pursue his lifelong passion. Counselors, teachers, and his environment discouraged a career in footwear design. His high school counselor encouraged him to go to the military. Similarly, his boss at McDonald's said designing footwear would lead him nowhere fast and encouraged him to stay there and work his way though the system, so he may eventually become a manager and make a $40,000 annual salary.

When D'Wayne was 16, his older brother Michael passed away and his mother encouraged him to get serious about his future. He always loved shoes but still didn't know what to do with that love. In 1988, at the age of 17, he entered a Reebok Design contest and won, but because he was too young and

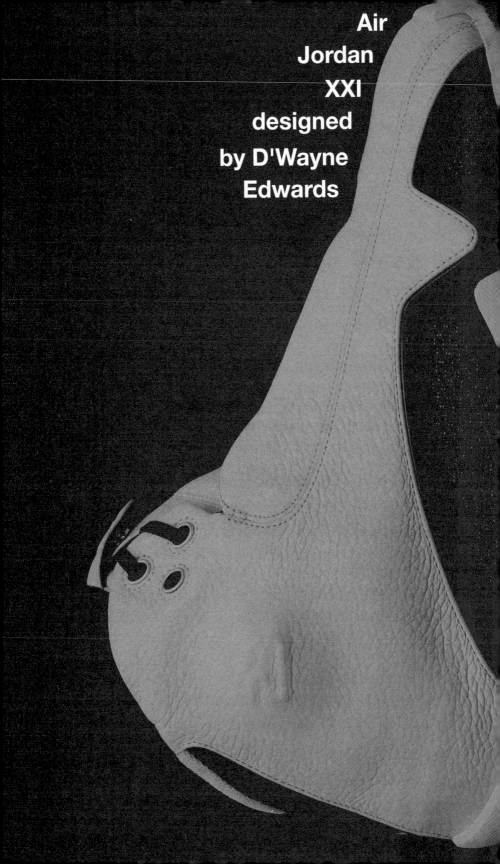

Air
Jordan
XXI
designed
by D'Wayne
Edwards

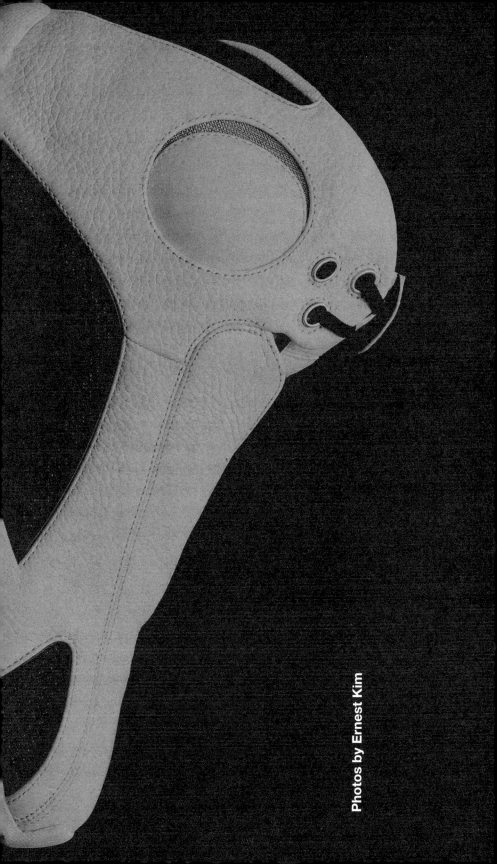

had no formal training, he was not hired. One day in 1989 his life would change. Through a temp agency, he was hired by L.A. Gear to work as a file clerk. For the next six months he tried desperately to get into the design department. During that six-month period, he put a sketch of a new shoe in the suggestion box every day. Finally, his work was noticed and he got a position as an entry-level designer.

In 1993, pioneer Karl Kani of Urban Fashion Designs sought D'Wayne to design his signature footwear collection licensed by Skechers USA. In 1998, as the Manager/Head Designer of the successful Karl Kani footwear label, Skechers USA offered D'Wayne his own footwear brand. He called it SITY, "city" spelled with an "S" for "style." In just one year, many of the top urban buyers were referring to SITY as the "freshest collection in years," and it was voted the number 2 brand to watch out for in 2000, behind Brand Jordan. In December of 1999, D'Wayne left Skechers USA, took a few months off, refreshed himself and reflected on his career. He remembered his dream at the age of 12 to be a footwear designer. The ultimate achievement of that dream would be a Nike footwear designer. In April of 2000, D'Wayne was hired by Nike's ACG's division in Beaverton, Oregon.

D'Wayne's career at Brand Jordan goes back to his beginning, when he was in high school sketching the Air Jordan II (AJ II) for fun. His first assignment with Brand Jordan was to design the NU Retro II (a remake of the AJ II). His footwear career had come full circle. D'Wayne had been a statistic his entire life. He went from being the product of a single parent household, a kid from Inglewood with an unrealistic dream, a McDonald's manager in the making, to being one of about 40 African-American footwear designers (there are approximately 600 footwear designers in the United States), to being one of six individuals to design the Brand Jordan line. He recently designed the Air Jordan XXI, which was released February 18, 2006, making him a part of footwear history.

A typical work week for D'Wayne may consist of a working meeting with Michael Jordan, Carmelo Anthony, or traveling around the globe (10 countries and 30 states to date) to create the fresh new concepts for Brand Jordan. He has come a long way from his day in Inglewood. D'Wayne has said working for Brand Jordan is not a job to him. It is his passion, something that he loves that he just happens to get paid for doing. He is using his God-given gifts to unlock his dreams, open doors, and work with arguably the greatest athlete of all time.

For D'Wayne, working for Brand Jordan has been the greatest segue into the world of branding. Michael Jordan is Brand Jordan. They are one. Brand Jordan has a soul and embodes excellence. D'Wayne Edwards is a brand, he has a soul and he embodies excellence. Two brands, one concep , the outcome: greatness. Incorporating passion into the process of developing your life plan is really about re-thinking who you are. In the next chapter we will apply what we have covered so far to the important task of understanding your mission.

Case Study
Malcolm Alexander, "Mr. Bobblehead"
Category: Leaper

Malcolm Alexander grew up in a small town of 1,200 people in Moruya, Australia. His career started at the Royal Military College in Duntroon, Australia's version of West Point. The Army recruiter offered him a $400 scholarship, which started him on a 13-year military career as a Special Air Service (SAS) agent: Captain of the Marine Counter-Terrorist Unit. When he met his wife he ended his military career with the highest seniority in his class.

He and his American wife headed to the United States to live in Chicago. He decided to start Alexander Promotions in 1996. The main function of his new company was importing logoed merchandise for corporations and sports teams. One phone call in 1999 would change the course of his company. The San Francisco Giants contacted him to manufacture Willie Mays bobbleheads. The goal was to recreate a theme from 1960, when the team had distributed bobbleheads. The initial order was for 35,000 bobbleheads. During the first meeting, although Malcolm had never seen or heard of a bobblehead, he agreed to the project and timing. He figured it wouldn't be a good idea to say no during the first meeting. He was determined to figure out how to manufacture the product. Since his top priority was getting his foot in the door with a high quality product, the profit margin on his first order was minimal (at best). Upon completion, he sent a bobblehead to every major league team.

The second year he secured orders from eight major league baseball teams. He now services the MLB, NBA, and the

NFL, with sales of 27 million units and growing. The timing was right — Beanie Babies and Pokémon had just run their course. The market was eager for the next new product. At a time when the latest trend was giving cost-effective souvenirs away to fans, the bobblehead grew hot. They are now high-end game give-a-ways, and even collectibles. Bronze Yankees replica bobbleheads are selling on eBay for over $200. Malcolm's product is being used as a prop in motion pictures and has started to populate secondary markets, such as the collector community and eBay.

In creating a successful brand, Alexander Promotions has focused on developing brand awareness with decision makers of professional sports and entertainment companies. Since he doesn't have the marketing budget of companies like Starbucks, Coca-Cola, or FedEx, Malcolm focuses on what he can control. He takes great pride in on-time delivery and exceeding his customers' expectations whenever possible. The distinction of Malcolm's bobbleheads is the quality and the life-like details of the product. Quality is a part of every phase of his product, including testing, safety standards, manufacturing, logistics, and delivery. With bobblehead competition all around him, Alexander's reputation is what has established him as a mover and shaker in the sports memorabilia industry.

Case Study
Oprah Winfrey
Category: Zoomer

Oprah has become an icon in American culture. Her brand centers around her talk show. There is a consistent message communicated between all of her entities: *O* magazine,

Harpo Productions, and *The Oprah Winfrey Show.*

Oprah Winfrey was born January 29, 1954, in Kosciusko, Mississippi. After a troubled adolescence in a small farming community, where she was sexually abused by a number of male relatives and friends of her mother, Vernita, she moved to Nashville to live with her father, Vernon, a barber and businessman. She entered Tennessee State University in 1971 and began working in radio and television broadcasting in Nashville. In 1976, Winfrey moved to Baltimore, where she hosted the TV chat show *People Are Talking.* The show became a hit and Winfrey stayed with it for eight years, after which she was recruited by a Chicago TV station to host her own morning show, *A.M. Chicago.* Her major competitor in the time slot was Phil Donahue, whose talk show was then the most successful in the nation. Within several months, Winfrey's open, warm-hearted personal style had won her 100,000 more viewers than Donahue and had taken her show from last place to first in the ratings. Her success led to nationwide fame and a role in Steven Spielberg's 1985 film *The Color Purple*, for which she was nominated for an Academy Award for Best Supporting Actress.

Winfrey launched *The Oprah Winfrey Show* in 1986 as a nationally syndicated program. With its placement on 120 channels and an audience of 10 million viewers, the show grossed $125 million by the end of its first year, of which Winfrey received $30 million. She soon gained ownership of the program from ABC, drawing it under the control of her new production company, Harpo ("Oprah" spelled backwards) Productions, and making more and more money from syndication.

In 1994, with talk shows becoming increasingly trashy and exploitative, Winfrey pledged to keep her show free of tabloid topics. Although ratings initially fell, she earned the respect of her viewers and was soon rewarded with an upsurge in popularity.

The media giant contributed immensely to the publishing world by launching her "Oprah's Book Club" as part of her talk show. The program propelled many unknown authors to the top of the bestseller lists and gave pleasure reading a new kind of popular prominence. In 2002, she concluded a deal with the network to air a prime-time complement to her syndicated talk show. Her highly successful monthly, *O: The Oprah Magazine*, debuted in 2000, and in 2004, she signed a new contract to continue *The Oprah Winfrey Show* through the 2010–11 season. The show is seen on 212 U.S. stations and in more than 100 countries worldwide.

Winfrey is a dedicated activist for children's rights; in 1994, President Clinton signed a bill into law that Winfrey had proposed to Congress, creating a nationwide database of convicted child abusers. She founded the Family for Better Lives Foundation and also contributes to her alma mater, Tennessee State University. In September 2002 Oprah was named the first recipient of The Academy of Television Arts & Sciences' Bob Hope Humanitarian Award. With all that Oprah has accomplished, she is foremost a talk show host. Her marketing message is consistent.

 Daily Download

Exercise #4: Identify your Brand YU category,
then describe your dream job.

Builder ☐

Leaper ☐

**Extreme
Leaper** ☐

Zoomer ☐

_____

_____

_____

_____

_____

_____

**"When purpose is unknown
abuse is inevitable."**

*—David Mayhem, founder,
Frontline Youth Communications*

Count the Cost

Shift 7

Authentic 9

Passion 1

Core 5

Mission 2

Voice 4

3°
Cost

03°

Plan for your success. Identify the cost, resources, and time it will take to successfully fulfill your mission. The passionate pursuit of the mission comes at a cost. Identify the cost and pay the price to bring the mission into view.

"The key is not to prioritize what's on your schedule, but to schedule your priorities."

—*Stephen R. Covey, author,*
The Seven Habits of Highly Effective People

5.05
Timing

"We cannot waste time.
We can only waste ourselves."
—*George Matthew Adams, author,* You Can

What will your personal brand look like in three, five, or ten years?
Highly successful organizations, teams, churches, companies,
and brands plan and strategize for the future. In the same way, we
each should have an individual plan (an i-Plan), one that structures
our time and helps us to achieve our mission.

"Objectives are not fate; they are directions. They are not com-
mands; they are commitments. They do not determine the future;
they are means to mobilize the resources and energies of the
business for the making of the future."
—*Peter Drucker, author,* The Daily Drucker

Setting objectives is important in planning. Planning helps to
shift life from an experiment to a series of structured events
that, when executed, produce desired results, just as organizations that are serious about success carefully structure and
execute their plans. For your individual success, it is
vital to understand the importance of planning and managing your life to yield the long-term results you seek.

Brand YU Plan

Your planning process should consist of documents that are flexible enough to adapt to shifts in direction, but concrete enough to provide solid direction that you understand and that you can communicate to yourself and to those with whom you interact in your professional life. The great nineteenth-century scientist Louis Pasteur said, "Chance favors the prepared person." In other words, timing is everything. People who are prepared can position themselves for great opportunities when they arise. Being prepared means making the best possible use of your time and not wasting it. I recently attended a workshop and one of the speakers made a statement that bears repeating: "The wealthy have the same amount of time as the poor. They don't have an extra second."

Time is the one commodity that you cannot retrieve once it has passed; those who master its uses are able to capitalize on key opportunities. One way to ensure that you use time as effectively as possible is to document what tasks you have to accomplish within a 24-hour period and to prioritize those tasks. The next step is to expand this practice to two days, three days, and so on. Research has shown that if you do something for 30 days straight it becomes a habit. Managing your time will allow you to balance work and leisure. Businesses set parameters for themselves and carefully manage them. As a mini-corporation, you have to manage your parameters as well. If your brand is developed through a series of assignments, brand planning is developed through a series of planning elements.

"Know thy time."
—Peter Drucker

Knowing your time requires more than a watch. It supercedes time zones, time standards, and work hours. Time is the currency of life; it is the medium of exchange. Time can be exchanged for anything in life. To produce a paycheck at the end of the week, you will have to exchange time for the required work. To produce a quality brand requires time. Your values are revealed by what you invest your time in or exchange your time for. Knowing thy time allows you to work with purpose to move and complete your assignment by focusing on placing yourself in position to completely, thoroughly, and effectively carry out every detail within a specified timeframe.

When Opportunity Knocks

In 1980, IBM approached Digital Research for a version of CP/M for its upcoming IBM PC. Legend has it that Gary Arlen Kildal, an early American microcomputer entrepreneur who created the CP/M operating system and founded Digital Research, Inc., snubbed the IBM representatives by going flying in his Pitts Special (an aerobatic biplane) for several hours. IBM related the story to Bill Gates, who was already providing the ROM BASIC interpreter for the PC, and Gates offered to provide an operating system as well, though he did not own one at the time. Seattle Computer Products was building a computer around the new Intel 8088 chip, and they needed an operating system for it. Tim Paterson, one of their employees, wrote QDOS, which stands for "Quick and Dirty Operating System." Gates obtained rights to it and licensed it to IBM, thus beginning MS-DOS/PC-DOS. Bill Gates had been IBM's second choice.

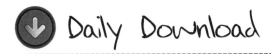 Daily Download

Exercise #5: Long-Term Planning

Timing is more a result of good planning than the result of luck. Planning is essential to establishing personal brand excellence in the perception of your target audience. To effectively plan your future, take your long-term plan (3 to 5 years out) and break it down into yearly goals, then into monthly, weekly, and daily goals. Take those daily goals and create a schedule for achieving them.

"We go to school to learn to work hard for money. I write books and create products that teach people how to have money work hard for them."

—*Robert T. Kiyosaki, author,* Rich Dad, Poor Dad

"Manhattan has the highest wealth disparity in the country. . . . Of Forbes 400 richest Americans (2006), 45 live in New York City, and they are each worth at least $1 billion. If our 45 billionaires suddenly decided to give half their collective $136 billion to the city's poor, each of the 1.5 million would get a check for more than $45,000."

—Henry Blodget, New York Magazine

financial integrity

"Pursuing your passion is fulfilling
and leads to financial freedom. "
   —Robert G. Allen, co-author,
   The One-Minute Millionaire

What is financial integrity? Ask Enron. Ask WorldCom. Ask Arthur Anderson. Why is there a need to have integrity as it relates to financial matters? How does this affect your personal brand? Your value system determines how you approach every area of your life. The lack of financial integrity contributes to many things— lost business opportunities and lost credibility, to name a few. In the case of Enron and the like, not only were the lives of the senior management affected, but so were the lives of employees, shareholders, vendors, and many families.

Just as finances are the lifeline of any business, an essential element of your personal brand is your financial stability, which can put you in a position to pursue business opportunities. As a one-person organization, you will find that limited capital resources can be one of the major challenges you must deal with. On the other hand, financial stability will allow you access to resources that can propel you to greatness.

Financial Aspects of Personal Branding

- Owner's Investment: Invest enough capital to ensure your future and your financial health.

- Operating Expenses: Cost control is an important function of every successful brand.

- System Value: The process of brand management is adding value while persuading the customer of the increased value in their life. It's what makes a customer pay more than the cost of raw materials. Manage your brand for increased value.

- Minimize Unpredictability: Having reserve funds available, back-up plans, and computer back-up files helps reduce unpredictability and the chaos it may create.

Business Brand Value

Brand value is one of the measures used to evaluate the worth of a brand. If a company's assets were liquidated and the only assets remaining were its trademarks, patents, intellectual property, and trade secrets, how much would the brand be worth? Similarly, if your work situation changed today and you were no longer employed or your business was dissolved, what would your market value be? If you retained your skills, educational degrees, and your work experience, how much would your intellectual properties and your brand be worth?

Interbrand is a leading marketing company that evaluates the world's most valuable brands, using a variety of criteria to rank them. To qualify for the Interbrand list, a brand must:

- Have a value greater than $1 billion.
- Derive about a third of its earnings outside its home country.
- Have publicly available marketing and financial data.

Even such heavyweights as Visa, Wal-Mart, Mars, and CNN are not on the list because they do not meet one or more of the three criteria. Parent companies are not ranked, which explains why Procter & Gamble is also not on the list. Airlines are not ranked because it is difficult to separate their brands' impact on sales from factors such as routes and schedules. Interbrand evaluates brands much the way analysts value other assets — on the basis of how much the companies are likely to earn in the future. Then the projected profits are discounted to a present value, based on the likelihood that those earnings will actually materialize. The first step is figuring out what percentage of a company's revenues can be credited to a brand. (The brand may be almost the entire company, as with McDonald's, or part of it, as in the case of Marlboro.) Based on reports from analysts at J.P. Morgan Chase, Citigroup, and Morgan Stanley, Interbrand projects five years of earnings and sales for the brand. It then deducts operating costs, taxes, and a charge for the capital employed to arrive at the intangible earnings.

The following table presents some of the top brands and their brand value.

Rank	Brand Name	Brand Value	Origin
1	Coca-Cola	$67.5B	U.S.
2	Microsoft	$59.9B	U.S.
7	Disney	$26.4B	U.S.
8	McDonald's	$26.0B	U.S.
42	IKEA	$7.8B	Sweden

Personal Brand Value

Interbrand may not be listing you, but as a brand you have brand value, skills, abilities, education, personal values, and work experience that potential employers or business partners will rank. The market that you live and work in and the types of services that you offer affect your brand value, and you can use your brand value to create personal wealth. Your personal brand value cannot be owned by a company; only you can own it.

Credit Score

In recent years, the way in which business is transacted has changed dramatically. Though employee screening has long been standard operating procedure in the financial world as a means of verifying the identity (name, address, and social security number) and credibility of applicants, an increasing number of other industries have also adopted the practice. A questionable credit history could make an individual competing for a position look less favorable. This reinforces one of the points concerning the management of your personal brand. Just as corporations and nonprofit organizations are held accountable to their stakeholders for their financial position, you as an individual must hold yourself accountable as well, proving your financial savvy and responsibility to would-be employers.

Corporations use the following financial measures to judge their financial success: gross profit, net income, ROI, stock prices, debt/liability ratios, and Dun & Bradstreet rating. The financial measures that affect you personally are: FICO score, credit history, debt/liability ratio, net worth, and liquid cash. (According to the Fair Credit Reporting Act (FRCA) an employer has to get written permission from a job applicant to run the credit check.)

The Brand YU mindset is one of overall health for your brand. As a personal brand, a person is a sum total of all the decisions that he or she has made over a lifetime. For some people that is good, but for others it may be a problem. The good news is that even bad decisions made in the past can usually be corrected.

Your Brand and Your Credit Report
An annual review of your credit report should be part of your financial planning. A credit report is a character report. It documents your creditability and character by detailing how well you fulfill your obligations. In other words, making and keeping your financial commitments can be viewed as a reflection of how you keep other commitments and the respect you have for others; it can affect how you are perceived by others. Your life cannot be compartmentalized; your work, life, and family are one continuum. Even if you feel secure in your current position and are not worried about your finances, it's important to always be aware that what is true today and important now can change dramatically within a short time. Therefore, when you think about your finances, be sure you prepare for unforeseeable future events and emergencies.

Budgeting for Personal Development
You need a budget. When you create it, you must know what revenues and expenditures to list for yourself. One essential expenditure should be a set amount of money each pay period for personal development. This is not reckless spending; instead, it is an investment in your brand. Examples of personal development include:

- Skills training (communication, software)
- Executive training
- Returning to college or earning an advanced degree
- Hiring consultants, such as career coaches

97

When it comes to investing in your personal development, you can use financial measures to evaluate your Personal Return On Investment (PROI). This is the return on your investment in education, training, and learning.

$$\text{Personal Return On Investment (PROI)} = \frac{\text{Revenue Generated}}{\text{Personal Dev. Cost}}$$

As a person your net worth, credit ratings, and salary can affect your ability to capitalize on business opportunities.

Benefits of Financial Integrity

The benefits of maintaining your financial integrity are many, and can allow you to:

- **Manage Perception:** Your private and public image must reflect each other. Future opportunities can be limited or eliminated based upon past decisions. Poor financial decisions can undermine future endeavors and present credibility.

- **Fund Valuable Initiatives:** As you develop and carry out your purpose future opportunities will make themselves available. Being in a position to capitalize will be decided by your financial position.

- **Increase Your Brand Value:** Your brand value increases and you are able to charge more for your services.

- **Increase Your Self Confidence:** Less debt and greater financial stability will increase the confidence of any person.

Re-thinking finances is more than just taking care of financial obligations. Your approach on how you handle finances impacts how you are perceived, how you are positioned for future opportunities, and the value of your brand.

Daily Download

Exercise #6: Pull an annual credit report (3-in-1) and review your credit history.

☐ **Completed**

04°

Give your brand a voice that communicates who you are through every human touch point and technology.

**"You have to defeat a great player's
aura more than his game."**

—Pat Riley, coach, Miami Heat

Know your competition

"You don't win silver, you lose gold."
—*Nike 1996 Olympic Games advertisement*

Competitiveness is hard wired into your DNA. Each one of us started life off as a winner competing against 300 million competitors to be born into this world. The world of branding is no less competitive. When it comes to competitors play to win, non-competitive people try not to lose. You must always play to win. In the process of developing your brand you will naturally have or create competitors. But if you respond effectively, rivalry will help to make you stronger, because it forces you to operate with a higher goal in mind and overcome complacency.

Knowing your competition is like playing a game. Every game has rules, a course, goals, and rivalries. To be competitive in a business, a game, a sporting event, or life in general, you have to understand the environment. Like a true leader, you must understand and consistently operate at a higher level than your competition.

Embrace Competition

Competition is often viewed as something negative, but it shouldn't be. Look at the results of competitive forces, innovation, and efficiency. Whether you realize it or not you need your competition — either competition against yourself or against another entity. Otherwise, you may not be prepared to compete in a world of downsizing, outsourcing, and global competition. No matter what field you are in, forces are competing for the same limited resources.

Competition forces you to streamline, focus, and operate in a way that positions your personal brand to be efficiently managed for growth and continued success. Challenges will keep coming up, but you must continue to elevate your game. You have to win internal battles before you compete externally. Accomplishing a personal goal, no matter how big or small, is a sign of success. It is a matter of perspective.

Global Competition

The competitive landscape has gone global and the intensity is only going to increase. No longer is your competition the person next door; you are now competing against someone in another country whose drive, passion, and technical competency may put him or her in a position to capture the opportunity or job that you desire. Just as businesses are re-thinking who they are and their business models you as an individual brand, a micro-company, must re-think your future. With the Internet, networking (social and technical), and technological advances, the world is shrinking. You are a click away from your closest competitor and your farthest customer. Every nation in the world is being affected and so are you.

Listed below are a few examples of what is happening:

- Nokia can develop cell phones for the Chinese market out of its product-design facility in Beijing.

- Toyota has set up a center for manufacturing small trucks in Thailand.

- Cisco is winning the most United States patents for new products at its Indian R&D operation.

- Basketball, once dominated by the United States, hasn't won the gold for the United States in the Olympics since 2000. The men's basketball team only lost two games in Olympic competition from 1936 to 2000. The overall Olympic record is 114 to 5 in Olympic games.

- China is producing more technical workers than the U.S.: 650,000 versus 220,000.

- India is producing 95,000 graduates in electrical engineering, information technology, and computer-science engineering. The U.S. produces 85,000 a year.

What Is Success to You?

Success is like a mistress to the average person, many people chase after her with an unclear picture of what she looks like or what true success is. Without a true understanding of true fulfillment and satisfaction, success can be elusive and eludes many people their whole life, in the quest to taste, touch, feel, see, or hear success. The masses sacrifice their future, families, and the things that are truly important and mean the most for a few seconds of glory. They chase after worthless pursuits to capture or become something that will ultimately become their demise. True success goes beyond chasing fantasies to pursuing visions that require patience, time, sacrifice, sweat, and tears. What is success to you? Is it some unrealistic man-made image that you entertain, or a solid, clear, concise vision that balances your core values, beliefs, and dreams? What does success look like? Success to someone who hasn't walked is taking that first step. Success to someone who hasn't talked is speaking that first word. Success is a matter of perspective. You are the picture of success.

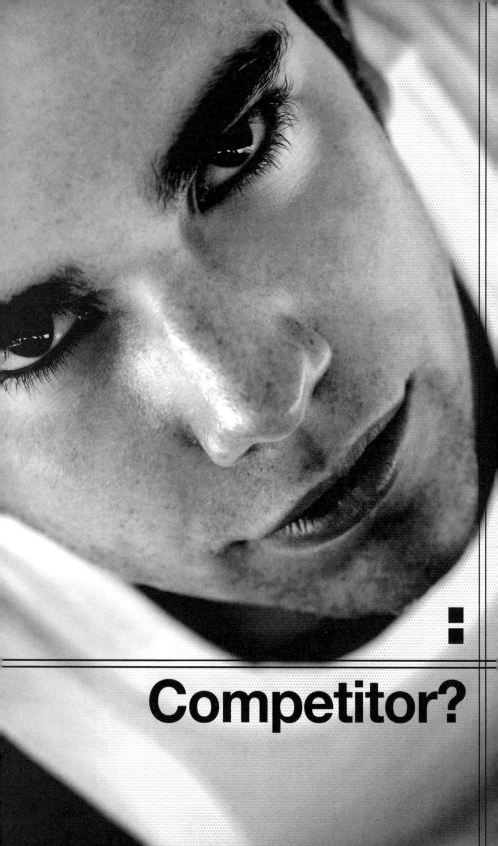

Competitor?

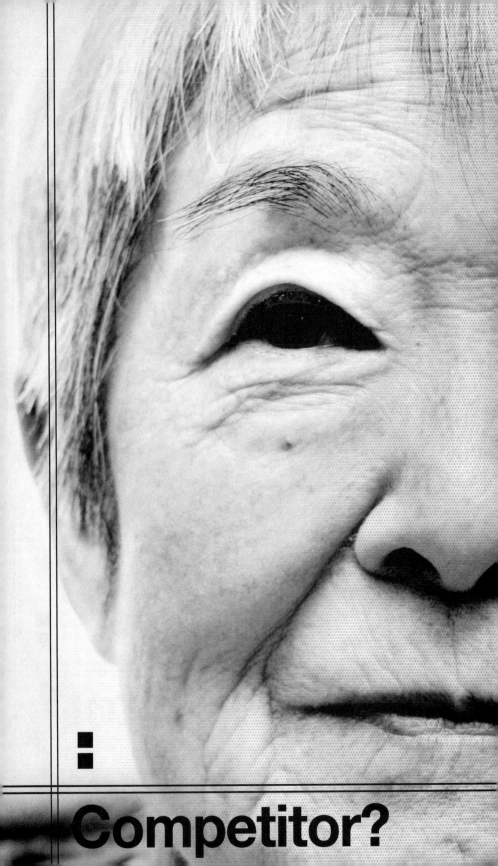

Competitor?

Competitor?

How will you keep up? Let's start by taking inventory of your current intellectual assets, skills, and abilities. It's time to think about what you have to offer.

Create a SWOT Analysis

A SWOT (Strengths, Weaknesses, Opportunities, and Threats) analysis allows you to think about your mission and how it applies to your career planning. It forces you to look at external forces that will affect your career direction. Listed below are some examples of each category.

Strengths
Strengths are your internal, positive attributes and selling points. You have some control over these. Examples include:

- Positive personal traits
- Relevant skills, competencies, knowledge, and work
- experience
- A solid education
- A strong network
- Commitment, enthusiasm, and passion for your field
- Understanding of your mission

Weaknesses
Weaknesses are your internal negative attributes. You have some control over these as well. Examples include:

- Undeveloped personal characteristics and poor work habits
- A lack of work experience or relevant experience
- No network or a limited one
- A lack of direction or focus
- Weak professional or career-management skills

- Education in a field that you don't like
- Poor computer literacy

Opportunities

Opportunities are uncontrollable external events that you can potentially leverage. Examples include:

- Favorable industry trends
- A booming economy
- A specific job opening
- An upcoming company project
- Emerging demand for a new skill or expertise
- Use of a new technology
- Referral to a high-powered contact

Threats

Threats are uncontrollable external factors that may work against you and require you to take protective action. Examples include:

- Industry restructuring and consolidation
- Changing market requirements and their impact on your employer
- Changing professional standards that you don't meet
- Reduced demand for one of your skills
- Evolving technologies you're unprepared for
- The emergence of a competitor, either to your company or to you personally
- A company decision-maker who does not like or support you

An external factor can sometimes be both a threat and an opportunity. For example, the emergence of a programming language that replaces one you know is a threat if you do nothing about it or an opportunity if you commit to becoming one of the early experts.

 Daily Download

Exercise #7: Complete a SWOT analysis.

Strengths	Weaknesses
Opportunities	**Threats**

You are never too young
to develop a personal brand.

**"What you do speaks so loudly that
I cannot hear what you say."**

—Ralph Waldo Emerson, American Poet

COMMUNICATION

"Think like a wise man but communicate in the language of the people."
—*William Butler Yeats, Irish poet*

Confidence. Confidence. Confidence. Its importance cannot be overstated. To be a leader and to develop your brand, you must demonstrate confidence in your dealings. People must have confidence in your abilities, services, and products before they develop a business relationship with you. Successful brands are made up of people who communicate effectively with one another. Ego can't play a role in the development of a brand, even when it's your ego. There is a fine line between confidence and arrogance. Being confident without becoming arrogant is a fundamental skill that you must hone.

Communication Is Key

Communicate. Communicate. Communicate. Effective branding requires effective communication. Defining and communicating your brand is mandatory. Even if you believe that you are not a charismatic person, you must communicate the attributes that make your brand unique and special. Suppose you are a shy person and think you have no talent at speaking in public. Even so, just about everyone has an innate ability to speak well — concisely, clearly, and with some humor — in public. In order to develop that trait and feel more comfortable with it, you must make a deliberate effort to do so. Take a class in public speaking, practice in front of family members, and just get out there and face the challenge of public speaking. The more you practice, the more confidence you will have in your skills as a public speaker. Just as a journey of a thousand miles begins with one step, your journey to effective speaking will start with one word. Once you have become an effective speaker, the next skill to master is to make sure that what you say is consistent with your mission. As the representation of Brand YU, it's important that you are capable of communicating accurate and compelling information about who you are.

Tips for Communicating Your Brand

To effectively communicate the appeal of Brand YU, you must:

- Change what you are saying. The power of your words begins the process of creating the image on the inside of you. It's essential that you develop your mission statement and a language that supports the brand and its direction.

- Increase the frequency of your brand communication. Keeping your message in front of your target market is key.

- Start now. The future is now, development is not a future project, it is a now project.

The Power of Your Words

Positive communication of your brand is important because every brand was started with words. Your ideas, word-of-mouth promotions, and product reviews are all brand builders or brand starters that are composed of words. Your words are powerful; they are building blocks to your future. As you hear your voice, your confidence in your ability to develop or improve yourself will increase. All successful brands have a voice. A commercial is nothing more than a voice repeated over and over and over.

Brand YU Confession

As a way of communicating the vision to yourself, develop a daily confession to internalize the message. Below is a sample Brand YU confession.

1. I have identified what I love to do and I am living my passion.
2. I understand my purpose and I have defined what I was created to accomplish.
3. I am who I say I am.
4. My success is planned and I prepare daily.
5. I am developing my skills, abilities, and talents daily to accomplish my mission.
6. My purpose is stronger than opposition, competition, and challenges.
7. My purpose is a force that is alive in me and propels me to the next step.
8. I speak my future, my mission, and my destiny daily.
9. I am bringing my future into the present and walking toward my destiny. I shall accomplish everything that I set my mind to do.
10. My future is bright and my destiny irrevocable. I am my brand.
11. I am my mission.
12. My mission is positioning me to generate wealth.

Types of Brand Communications

Just as with any other type of communication, brand communication can be achieved in the following ways, either alone or in combination.

- **Verbal:** You are the head marketer for your brand and must speak effectively in phone calls, in one-to-one interviews, and in making presentations at meetings.

- **Written:** It is critical to be clear and avoid sloppy errors in e-mails and typed documents, such as reports and overhead presentations. Written communications are permanent records of your brand's integrity.

- **Nonverbal:** Communication without words includes body language, such as gestures and posture, facial expressions, and eye contact. A smile now at the appropriate moments time goes a long way.

This table illustrates the communication tools of business brands and personal brands

Business Brands	vs.	Personal Brands
• PR • Advertising • Marketing • Corporate Web site • Media planning • Packaging	comparison	• Networking • Resume • Web presence • Name recognition • Style/clothes • Appearance

Marketing Your Brand

How will you market your brand? Among the vehicles you can use are the Internet, web sites, your resume, and press kits. Brand YU might be highly effective, but you still have to sell yourself and your ideas. Create an internal PR system that communicates a single message.

The crucial components of marketing are:

- a single, unified message
- truth in advertising
- consistency of repetition

In marketing, communicating a single message is critical. Oprah Winfrey is a classic example of someone who communicates a single message through her personal brand. She never dilutes her message by claiming that she is an expert in medicine, auto racing, or farming, for example. Her expertise is in being a talk show host who is concerned with the issues of our time—and that is her message. Similarly, everything that you do or say should communicate information about your brand. Oprah Winfrey's story tells how one person developed a successful brand by staying true to her message.

Be a Brand Evangelist

Advertising and marketing have shifted. Traditional channels are not the only or most effective ways to promote your brand. The shift favors individual and smaller institutions; the cost and effectiveness is more in line with allowing all businesses or organizations to use them. Evangelism is usually, but not always, related to the Word of God. In cultivating brand evangelism, companies, organizations and people promote the good news and the truth of their brand to the masses. This is especially appropriate when a product or service has a profound impact on people's lives. You are the evangelist for Brand YU.

In the same way that leadership skills can be cultivated, so can the art of communication — of being an evangelist for your brand. You may be the most intelligent person with the greatest ideas, but you limit your opportunities if you can't communicate them. Communicating Brand YU to your target audience consistently and with a single message is critical to your success. According to prwebdirect.com, "BzzAgent, Inc. is a word-of-mouth marketing and research firm located in Boston, Massachusetts, founded by Dave Balter, author of *Grapevine: The New Art of Word-of-Mouth Marketing*, whose network of volunteer brand evangelists shares their honest opinions about products and services with other consumers. The company's proprietary process and system, the BzzEngine, allows them to provide diligent, systematized, and measurable word-of-mouth marketing campaigns. Clients include Penguin Putnam Publishing, Ralph Lauren, SC Johnson, Kellogg's, and Anheuser-Busch. "

The Elevator Speech

In order to successfully market Brand YU, you must be able to express your mission in 25 words or less, or clearly communicate it in 30-seconds. This concept is referred to as the "elevator speech," meaning that if you were on an elevator and had only the length of the trip from floor 1 to floor 10 to promote yourself to someone, what would you say? The elevator speech is your audible mission statement. It must tell:

- who you are
- what you do
- what makes you unique
- what need you fulfill

Being able to state this on command is an invaluable skill.

Daily Download

> **Exercise #8: Create your elevator speech.**
>
> _____
>
> _____
>
> _____
>
> _____
>
> _____
>
> _____
>
> _____
>
> _____
>
> _____
>
> _____

05

Develop yourself from the inside out. Sustained development starts internally and drives what is externally exposed. Mental, spiritual, and physical development, as well as a foundation of character and values, creates the image we see.

**"A goal is a planned conflict
with the status quo."**

*—Hyrum W. Smith,
Creator of the Franklin Day Planner*

core components

"Nearly all men can stand adversity, but
if you want to test a man's character, give him power."
—*Abraham Lincoln, 16th U.S. President*

I believe that every brand has a mind, body, and spirit. In distinguishing yourself through your personal brand, it is vital to establish that core (mind, body, and spirit). A personal brand taps into the very essence of who you. Developing your core is about adding value.

Inside-Out Thinking

Our society thinks in reverse, outside in. Inside out thinking is re-thinking how you approach development, focusing on development of values, character, and intellect. All of these things are learned behaviors. Each person makes a decision to live and act a certain way. Everything starts from the inside, or at the core. Changing what is on the inside will lead to improvements on the outside. The investment is exchanging the currency of time to build up your core elements.

Each one of us has a worldview, the lens through which we see life. Your core is magnified to reveal your true moral character and approach to life. Your life cannot be compartmentalized; a lack of discipline in one area can lead to out-of-control conditions in other areas. The effort that you put into your physical conditioning, mental development, character development, and living your values are inextricably bound to your personal brand. Life is full of decision-making opportunities, and every day you are making decisions that either drive you toward your mission or away from it and from the development of your true core identity.

Creating Excellence

Great leaders realize that their physical and mental conditioning can have a direct impact on their effectiveness. You will command a higher level of respect when you have conditioned yourself to be a world-class leader. This begins with mental development that creates competence and an understanding of the elements that compel and drive success in your industry. Appropriate physical conditioning means understanding and properly taking care of your body. Creating a positive lifestyle, setting healthy boundaries, and establishing high goals are important parts of that. Your personal condition, both physical and mental, should be planned and deliberate, never accidental. Your brand will reach a level of excellence because you thought through and implemented a personal plan; it will not happen by chance.

Brand YU leaders are driven by their belief in themselves, not by a desire to impress others. They embrace substance over style. What is the purpose of what you are doing? What do you do better than anyone else? The key is to focus on your strengths rather than on your weaknesses. Identify and develop your values. How critical are your values to your brand? Are you willing to compromise them? Your values should dictate what approach your brand will take, and you should be prepared to decline projects and job opportunities that are not harmonious with your values.

Inner Development: The Soul of Your Brand

Your brand cannot be separated from you. Your character, values, and the way you live your life all reflect on your brand and comprise elements of the brand's identity.

> **"Character of an organization should start with and be embodied in the leadership. . . . Brands rise and fall in connection with the reputation of their leadership. It's not about building creditability, but being creditable, and in the real world of branding the leadership is an extension of the brand. You are not only an extension, you are the brand. Brands of the now and the future will require leaders of high-moral fiber. Who you are and your value system will permeate through your brand. ... The late business leader Bernard M. Baruch once noted that none of the technological revolutions he witnessed in his lifetime did away with the need for character in the individual or the ability to think."**
>
> —*Jeffrey Cufaude, founder of Idea Architects*

> **"Trust is the foundation of leadership. To build trust, a leader must exemplify these qualities: competence, connection, and character. People will forgive occasional mistakes based on ability . . . but they won't trust someone who has slips in character. . . . Character and leadership credibility go hand in hand."**
>
> —*John Maxwell, author,* The 21 Irrefutable Laws of Leadership

You cannot hide who you are, and you must be consistent in the image you project and the values you embody. Consistent behavior is essential. Brand YU is built on trust: trust that you are who you say you are, trust that you have the skills that you claim to have, trust that you will keep the promises that you made in your marketing message.

Character is the foundation of your brand, because your character influences every aspect of your life. Thus, when you make a commitment or give your word you must be ready to fulfill your promise. Therefore,

- Think before you commit.
- Do not promise what you cannot realistically deliver.
- Undercommit and overperform.

Grow Your Core

Character

What is character? Character is defined as who we really are and how we act when no one is watching. Corporations are being required (post Enron) to behave responsibly, to have a defined philosophy and a code of ethics. Of course, these qualities are not only for corporations. Your personal brand mandates that you have a high moral character, that you live according to a defined set of values, and dedicate yourself to a meaningful purpose. By understanding and embracing these traits, you can position Brand YU to be respected and sought after.

In 2002, corporate America faced a reckoning. Enron, WorldCom, and several other large corporations were exposed for having failed to be "good corporate citizens." In the November 5, 2004 issue of *USA Today,* an article by Jayne O'Donnell and Greg Farrell read "Business Scandals Prompt Look into Personal Lives." The article pointed out that, in a quest for more ethical leaders, recruiters are looking into executives' personal lives for evidence of what the recruiters consider to be misbehavior. For example, discovering that a prospective executive has had an extramarital affair may raise questions about his or her integrity. While there's no scientific proof that a philanderer is more likely to be involved in financial fraud, many executives implicated in recent corporate scandals had been engaged in other forms of questionable moral behavior in the past.

Society rewards style versus substance, charisma versus character. This unbalanced process breeds self-indulgence and drives a person to focus on self-satisfaction regardless of the price. Undeveloped character allows a person to view possessions, popularity, power, prestige, and people inappropriately. No leader can afford to do without self-discipline; the cost of a lack of self-discipline is too high. As you develop and rise in leadership, strong moral character becomes a fundamental asset and is vital to your success and a challenge to maintain. The reality is that we live in an age where outsourcing is a way of life. Any task that can be performed quicker or cheaper is a candidate for outsourcing. But while you can outsource jobs, assignments, and tasks, you cannot outsource character. It's up to you to maintain strong character, for yourself and all those you lead. Character extends beyond just integrity, and includes creativity, excellence, competence, and responsibility, among other traits.

What industry doesn't require character? Athletics, politics, ministry, law, medicine, automotive, journalism? Every field is impacted by the character of those who comprise that field. Can character be developed? Of course, but this is a process that requires time and discipline. As long as you are willing to invest the time and to take a disciplined approach, you can expect to develop the kind of character that you can take pride in.

"Character is doing the right thing when nobody's looking. There are too many people who think that the only thing that's right is to get by, and the only thing that's wrong is to get caught."

—J. C. Watts, Former U.S. Representative, Oklahoma, 4th District

Mental Development: The Mind of the Brand

Going to school is an apt metaphor for improving Brand YU. Are you ready to go to school? Whether or not you are enrolled in an institution of higher learning, you are in school. We are all in a worldwide classroom. Class is in session every day.

Where do you choose to sit in class? Do you take the challenging assignments? Do you try to get by or are you trying to excel? Training to be world class in your field is important. Whether you enroll in a seminar, a night class, an ivy league institution, or simply choose to continue learning by reading books, journals, and gathering information online, you can commit to being a lifelong learner. Commit to reading, create a love for learning and reading, become a strategic thinker, learn to engage both sides of your mind. You can turn yourself into an expert—one whom others turn to as a reliable source of information and advice in a particular area.

Rethinking mental development. What does it mean to be smart? What does it mean to be smarter than someone else? In fact how do you quantify being smarter? It is GPA? Is it IQ? Is it your career field? Is it how much you make? Is it power? Is it influence? Being smart is effectively using resources to get desired results. Obviously, reading alone, going to school, or acquiring information doesn't necessarily mean an individual is smart. Utilization of acquired information to produce desired results requires an individual to think about what he or she is doing to structure or convert the information into something useful better known as *work*. Smart people think and process information to creatively solve problems and capitalize on business opportunities. Your personal brand should be run like a business. Every successful business has a set of competencies. What are the core competencies of your personal brand? Think about what they are and then look to further develop them.

Studies have shown that the average person uses only 10 percent of his or her brain capacity. This is an inefficient use of our intellectual capacities. Commit yourself to constant learning and to thinking with openness to new ideas, new ways of doing things. Open yourself up to new experiences as a way to gain knowledge. Understand the value of your experience; some of the greatest lessons are learned in unexpected places. Decide to actively acquire knowledge.

> **"Perhaps the most valuable result of all education is the ability to make yourself do the thing you have to do, when it ought to be done, whether you like it or not; it is the first lesson that ought to be learned; and however early a man's training begins, it is probably the last lesson that he learns thoroughly."**
> —*Thomas H. Huxley, English biologist (1825–1895)*

Double-Minded

The future of branding is in utilizing the left and right side of your brain. Work is taking on a different meaning. U.S. corporations are outsourcing functions for IT, engineering, and manufacturing. People who can fulfill functions are available in emerging markets (Asia, China, and elsewhere). The phrase double-minded traditionally meant to be unstable or to constantly change your mind. Brand YU's connotation of double-minded means using the left side (logic) and the right side (creative) of your brain. Your passion helps you to creatively do this.

Physical Development: The Body of the Brand

Today, we live in a world that is skin deep. Magazine covers, movies, and product commercials are littered with models, celebrities, movie stars and the moving target of what society says is in and is beautiful. As a culture we are obsessed with the habits and lifestyles of the rich and famous. Since physical interaction is a function of life and business, you can't ignore or avoid this fact. Packaging and physical development is an important part of your personal brand and must be addressed. As a personal brand, product design is essential.

> **"For business, it's no longer enough to create a product that's reasonably priced and adequately functional. It must also be beautiful, unique, and meaningful"**
> —*Daniel H. Pink, author,* A Whole New Mind

How many people are obsessed with beautiful design? People are willing to spend more for a product that is designed well. If you are competing against someone else and all things are equal, presentation can be a deciding factor. How many times have you been in a store holding two products in your hand and ultimately chose one product over the other because of the design? Beautiful design is in the eye of the beholder. Have you creatively thought about how you can incorporate design into your life? Outer development is one of the three areas of developing your brand.

- What does beautiful design look like?
- How do you know when you have experienced it?
- How can you incorporate design into your life?
- Is design beautiful to everyone?

Niche or targeted products don't appeal to everyone, nor are they created for everyone. Understand that you are uniquely designed regardless of today's ever changing standards.

Exotic flower.
Is this flower beautiful?

Exotic bird.
Is this animal beautiful?

135

Modern Living.
Is this living room beautiful?

Vintage Car.
Is this car beautiful?

The images in the previous pictures are beautiful to some people and mean little to others. Throughout this book we covered inside-out development— developing who you are from the inside-out— so you can address the areas of Brand YU that you control. Think about three points as you approach personal product design.

- **Designer Genes.** Your structure, physical make-up, and personality are an important part of your personal product design. Your skin color, your hair, your voice, and your style are all a part of your personal product design. You are distinctive. Your success is in your genes.

- **Niche Product Design.** You can't be all things to all people. There is something uncommon about you that is tailored to the way you are wired.

- **33.3%.** Complete the circle: mental, inner, and outer development. One-third of your development (on the outside) reveals what you have been doing with the other two-thirds (on the inside). Be the best that you can be. Use outward development as an opportunity not an obstacle to define who you are. We live in a real world.

Tiger, the Physical Brand

The body of the brand of Eldrick (Tiger) Woods has revolutionized the sport of golf. He began his professional golf career in 1995. Since then, his dominance has been such that Woods won 52 percent of all the prize money he could have won. Golf had traditionally been a sport that didn't require a lot of physical development. Now we see how one individual can radically change a sport, as Tiger Woods did, or even an industry. It is necessary to do weightlifting, training, and physical conditioning to be a successful competitor, even in golf. How can proper physical conditioning give you an advantage in your industry? How important is product design to personal brand management?

You don't have to be a professional athlete to benefit from physical conditioning. Being physically fit and agile can help you become more efficient and able to accomplish more. This does not only mean following an exercise regimen; it also means living a healthy lifestyle in every way. Physical development and fitness is about establishing healthy boundaries and being responsible for your body.

Taking care of your body not only helps keep you fit for the challenges of the business world, it also tells your colleagues, competitors, and customers that you are a disciplined person, in control of your life. In the same way, the way you dress also tells people a lot about you. Like it or not, people will initially judge you by your appearance. Therefore, always present the best possible image. Look your best. Dress for the position you are seeking. Remember that you represent Brand YU.

When you think of beautiful design, think about the products and environment they resonate with. Don't consume yourself with tangibles you can't change or unrealistic expectations.

Physical development is a critical part of your brand's development. As a beautifully designed product, the overall health of a personal brand takes on a different meaning. This means that to be a successful brand you must also achieve a healthy, physically fit lifestyle.

Being world-class means preparing yourself to be world-class.

 Daily Download

---

Exercise #9: List three steps that you will take to enhance your mental, physical, and inner development.

Mental development

1. _____

2. _____

3. _____

Physical development

1. _____

2. _____

3. _____

Inner development

1. _____

2. _____

3. _____

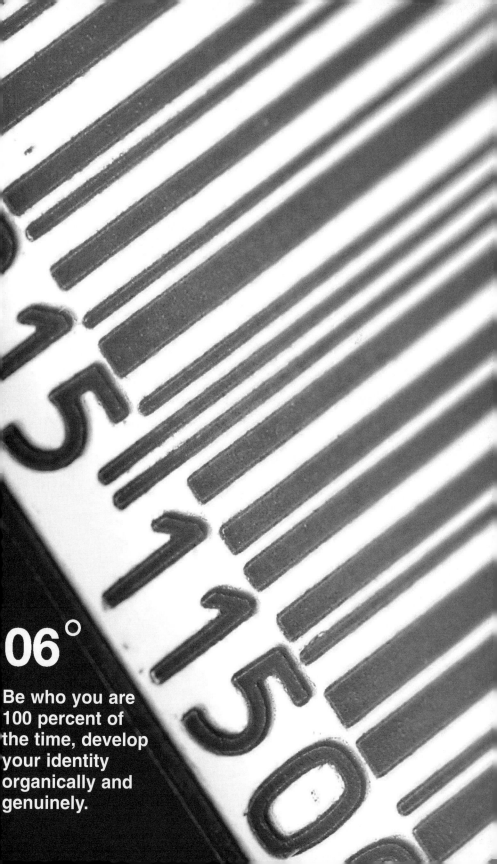

06°

Be who you are
100 percent of
the time, develop
your identity
organically and
genuinely.

"A brand for a company is like a reputation for a person. You earn reputation by trying to do hard things well."

—Jeff Bezos, founder, Amazon.com

brand dna

"I spend a major part of my waking hours making things that no one needs. After all, fashion is just clothes, just shoes. Fashion doesn't really change the world."

—*Kenneth Cole, American shoe manufacturer*

It's time to develop a healthy identity through branding. This chapter is about developing your brand naturally and organically, free from artificial colors, flavors, and the bitter taste that will contaminate or dissipate the identity of your brand. Brand identity communicates an entity's core values, credibility, associations, encompasses relationships, personality, and corporate culture. Brand identity includes the visual and audible elements that enable others to recognize a brand (stationery, signage, logo type, mark, service, and packaging).

The Building Blocks of a Brand

DNA (deoxyribonucleic acid) is the most important part of chromosomes. It carries genetic information. In recent years, law enforcement officials have found it to be invaluable as a method of identifying criminals. No two people have the same DNA. Your DNA makes you totally unique among the 6.5 billion people who exist on Earth. If you stop and think about this, it's truly an amazing fact. But the fact that you are different doesn't mean anything if you are unable to harness and communicate the differences in a way that helps you achieve your life's purpose.

In much the same way, the DNA of a brand identifies who or what the brand is and what makes it unique. The DNA, or unique attributes, of a brand helps to differentiate it from products or services that appear similar. Brand identification is how your brand is perceived by others, those who are drawn to it because of the specific needs, real or perceived, it meets.

A brand is not just a symbol or a logo, a brand has a personality that implies a defined set of expectations and promises. For example, the FedEx brand is associated with guaranteed delivery, and the Nordstrom brand means personal service. In creating Brand YU, you must ensure that the brand resonates with your lifestyle and identity.

Although most people think identity is what people see, the root of identity is what one develops on the inside, which is then manifested on the outside. It is what people don't see that constitutes the root of identity. This means that your thoughts, words, character, and values create the exposed elements of your identity, the part is seen by others. To change who you truly are, a transformation of your thoughts, words, character, and values is required. Yes, you can change your external traits and affect others' perception of you, but truly changing your identity goes deeper than making exterior changes.

Creating an Online Identity

An important component of brand identity is the online one — for individuals as well as corporations. Internet marketing and an online identity are critical in this day and age. Your audience can learn about your online identity through:

- **Online searches:** In the Internet age online identity is an important aspect to consider. The first step that most people and companies take to learn more about a person is to conduct online research through search engines such as Google.

- **Online presence:** Creating an Internet presence can be an effective way to position and communicate who you are and to target your audience. There are many popular ways to market yourself online, including personal web sites, blogs, and job web sites, such as monster.com.

Water, Water Everywhere

What is the most essential thing you need to survive? Water. It is basic to life and its unique properties are required for all living things. Some organisms consist of 90 percent water. Humans are made of 60 percent water. A person can only survive without water for three days, though some survivors of natural disasters or accidents have miraculously lived longer.

Water is a unique substance that in solid form is less dense than in liquid form. This is the reason ice floats when it is in water. Similarly, when brand identity is solid it causes you to rise and float above the competition. In the same way that water is essential to life, brand identity is essential to the life of your brand.

Before the U.S. Congress passed the Safe Drinking Water Act in 1974, most people drank water from the tap or from fountains. A few companies sold distilled or filtered water, primarily to businesses. After the law was passed, bottled water became more commonly used. An industry was created to sell a commodity that was readily and inexpensively available to most people in the United States. By the 1980s, it had become chic to drink bottled water. Today, bottled water is a multi-billion dollar industry. How was demand created to sell a product that we already had access to readily and freely?

There are more than 200 brands of bottled water worldwide. The major brands include Aquafina, Dasani, Voss, Evian, and Fiji (bottled water from the Fiji Islands). Studies have shown that customers perceive bottled water as tasting better and being cleaner, more pure, and healthier than tap water. The goal of selling standard bottled water (not the enhanced water, which can include flavors, vitamins, minerals, and electrolytes) is to convince customers to buy a product they don't need to buy.

Great numbers of people have bought into the idea of drinking bottled water. Most brands of bottled waters taste the same. So what distinguishes one from the other? Is it the shape of the bottle? Is it the sound the bottle makes as it is opened? Are there significant differences in how the water is filtered, processed, and packaged? Do these processes affect the flavor, taste, color, or cleanliness? How does all this affect the decision to buy a particular brand?

If water can be differentiated and packaged uniquely to target a specific market, then so can your personal brand. The beverage industry works hard to market a product whose characteristics for the most part are indistinguishable from brand to brand. But consumers still choose one brand over another because they like it better. In the same way, your brand can be distinguished from other, seemingly similar, brands. It's up to you, however, to ensure that your brand stands out against the competition and is perceived by your potential market to be the superior one.

Standing Out

Customization reigns supreme in our global society. Almost anything can be customized: your sneakers (at nikeid.com), ring tones for your cell phone (at verizonwireless.com), and so on. One entrepreneur I know uses a specific color paper clip to distinguish herself from her competitors. This seemingly inconsequential detail differentiates her paper-clipped proposals and gives her a presence even when she is not present. If you're one of those people who say, "I am not creative or clever, I have never designed anything," learn to think way beyond the obvious when developing your personal brand. Pursue projects that are outside the requirements of your job and complete them with extra effort and creativity. The design of your life brand should be authentic and should reflect you. It should reveal the real you.

Personal Packaging

**"Clothes don't make the man, but they
go a long way towards making the businessman."**

—Thomas J. Watson Jr., former CEO of IBM

Are you packaged for success? Successful personal packaging requires an understanding of the culture and the code of conduct for your profession or industry. Thus, how you dress, speak, and act are important components of your brand identity. Just as packaging is an essential component of the way in which corporations market their product—whether the product is bottled water, shoes, or computer software—your personal packaging is an inextricable component of your brand identity and the marketing of your personal brand. Developing your physical presentation is important in creating your personal brand. Further, your personal packaging must consistently present a professional, polished, successful image to your market. A key element in branding is consistency—consistency of thought, presentation, mission, personal packaging, products, and services.

Personal Packaging and Your Appearance. The purpose of personal packaging is to attract the attention of your target audience and create a particular image. What you wear communicates your brand and who you are. Every profession has a culture. At the time you decided to pursue a career in your field, you most likely accepted all that being in the profession entailed.

Is your appearance consistent with your profession? Is your appearance consistent with your brand and its values? If you answered no to either of those questions, here is an opportunity to raise your profile. How important is your appearance in relation to your brand? If face-to-face meetings and in-person interaction with customers are a part of your professional role, your physical appearance — how you dress, your posture, your mannerisms—become of the utmost importance. The visual impressions that you communicate will either undermine or complement your other branding elements. Are you packaged for success?

The following table compares the perceived traits, or images, between business and personal brands.

Business Brands	Traits
• Nike • Harley-Davison • eBay	• Athletic • Rugged • Thrifty
Personal Brand	**Traits**
• Brand YU	• Competent • Genuine • Punctual • Dependable • Trustworthy • Credible

Personal Packaging and Your Personality. Every brand has a personality. What is your brand's personality? Your personality dramatically affects how you interact with others. Do you draw customers to your product or direct them away? Your customers will perceive your brand personality based on their experiences with you — in phone conversations, on your web site, or in person — whenever they utilize your services. Therefore, it is important that your personality is warm and accessible, and draws others to your brand. This does not mean you should become someone you are not; however, if you are aware of certain personality traits or characteristics in yourself that impede the success of your brand, it is within your power to change them.

Imagine how a brand's personality would think, feel, and act if it were human. What personality traits would you like to have associated with your brand? Every detail associated with your brand establishes your mark on the business world and life. Authenticity is the greatest tool that you can utilize in developing your brand DNA. Identify your three favorite brands. What characteristics make them your favorites? Do a product analysis of yourself and identify your three favorite characteristics.

Daily Download

Exercise #10: Complete the Brand YU Water Theory Worksheet.

Completed ☐

Brand YU Water Theory
Group Exercise

The Brand
YU Life

Name _____

Brand Name _____ Date _____

Purpose
The purpose of this group exercise is to create a brand of bottled water and identify the distinguishable characteristics of your brand of bottled water.

Equipment   1- Label   1-Bottle of Water   1- Marker   1- Scissors

Brand Name _____

Price Point _____

Target Audience _____

Distinguishable Features_____

_____

_____

_____

_____

_____

Packaging _____

_____

_____

Brand Promise _____

_____

Goal:
There are currently 200+ brands of bottled water with distinguishable features, identify your unique differences.

"Disneyland is a work of love. We didn't go into Disneyland just with the idea of making money."

—Walt Disney

C. 11.
PLAY

"My whole life is one big bucket of fun!"
-Sheryl Crow, Musician

Have some fun. Be a kid again. Live life to the fullest.

Has time expired on your vision?

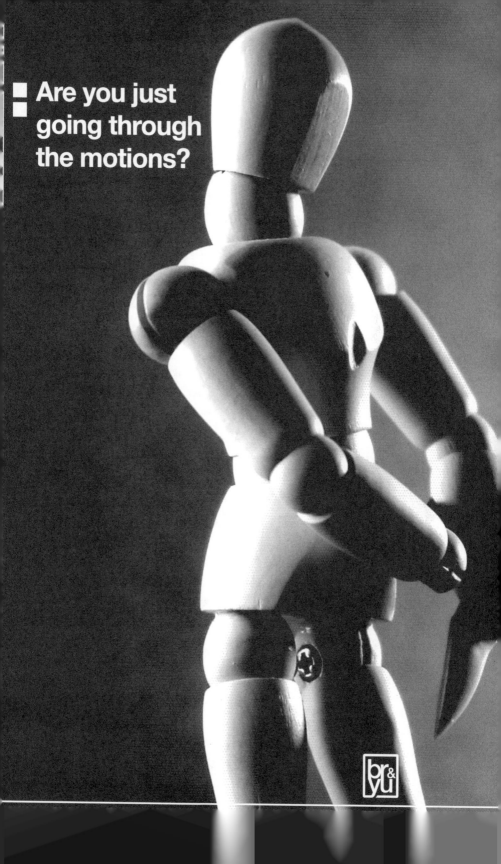

▋ Are you tired of playing games?

It s not over.

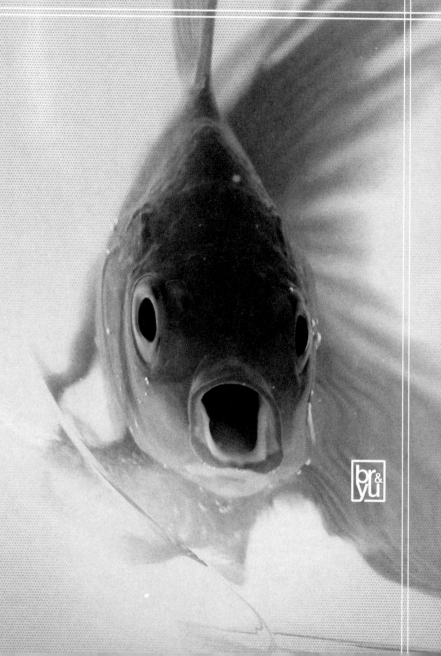

Be Hungry.

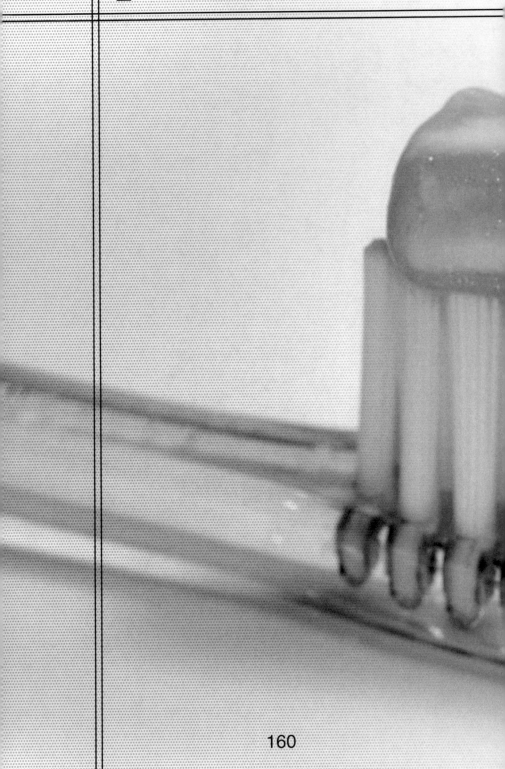

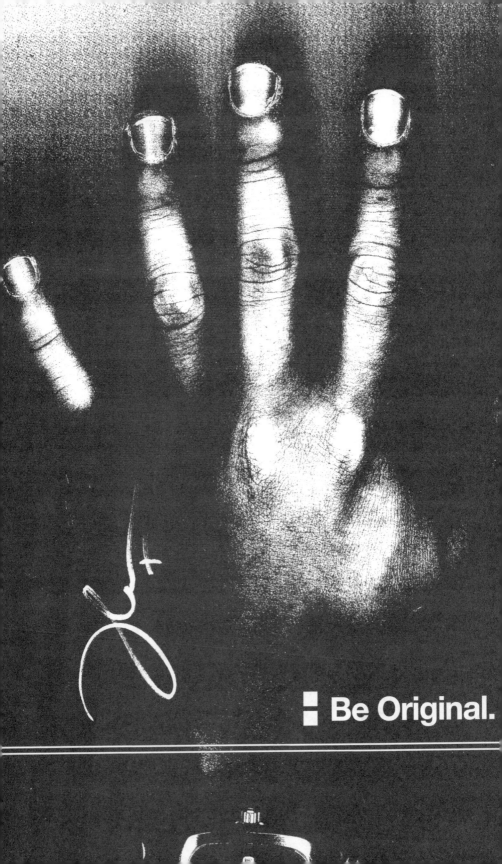

Be Original.

■ Be Cool.

*Not actual size: Object is cooler than it appears.

▉ Be Different.

Write down one way to apply each instruction as it relates to personal branding.

Be Hungry.

_____

_____

Be Fresh.

_____

_____

Be Cool.

_____

_____

Be Original.

_____

_____

■ Don't wait until you are famous or wealthy.

Practice your signature now.

example

Author & Mogul

Hajj Flemings

Directions:
Grab a pen and practice your signature. Make it distinctive.

_____

_____

_____

 Daily Download

Exercise #11: Create your signature.

_____

_____

_____

"I am the greatest, I said that even before I knew I was."

—Muhammad Ali,
Former Heavyweight Champion

"They did it! YouTube bought by Google for $1.65B in less than two years."

—Matt Marshall, Venturebeat.com

digital age

"Digital speed shrinks the distance between the information and the decision."

—*George Stalk, Jr., author*, Hardball:
Are You Playing to Play or Playing to Win?

We live in an on-demand, wireless society that never sleeps, where business is transacted 24 hours a day, 7 days a week. The speed of business is increasing at an alarming rate. In this ever-expanding and ever-changing climate, it is important to understand technology and make it work to your advantage. The Internet has removed many economic barriers that previously prevented people from pursuing career opportunities and businesses from initiating ventures and increasing the awareness of their brand. Disregarding technology is not an option for Brand YU'ers. The affordability of networking hardware and telecommunication devices makes them viable for just about everyone. Even young people barely old enough to vote are savvy enough to take advantage of the opportunities technology offers.

The Million Dollar Homepage (www.milliondollarhomepage.com) is a Web site conceived by Alex Tew, a 21-year-old student from Wiltshire, England, to help raise money for his university education. Launched on August 26, 2005, the Web site is said to have generated a gross income of $1,037,100 (U.S. dollars) and has a Google page rank of 7. The index page of the site consists of a 1000 x 1000 pixel grid (one million pixels), on which Tew sells image-based links for $1 per pixel, in minimum ten-by-ten blocks. A person who buys one or more of these pixel blocks can design a tiny image which will be displayed on them, and can also have the image link to a URL. In addition, a slogan of the block owner's choosing is displayed when a web surfer's cursor is over the link. The aim of the site was to sell all of the pixels in the image, thus generating $1 million dollars of income for the creator. On January 1, 2006, the remaining 1,000 pixels were put up for auction on eBay. The auction closed on January 11 with the winning bid of $38,100.00. This brought the final tally to $1,037,100 in gross income.

Unlimited Access

According to a yearlong study by a team from McKinsey & Co. — a study involving 77 companies and almost 6,000 managers and executives — the most important corporate resource over the next 20 years will be the talent of technologically literate, globally astute, and operationally agile, smart, and sophisticated business people. Technology is a means of acquiring and providing access to your brand. Most successful brands have a web presence. The web can be used as a tool to market what you do. Just look at a couple of statistics about how the Internet has become a staple of daily living.

- Eighty percent of Internet users have looked for answers to specific questions about a broad variety of issues, from health care to religion to news.

- Eighty-eight percent of Americans who go online say the Internet plays a role in their daily routines.

Where do you go for information about your favorite brand? Instead of calling customer service, you likely turn to the Internet. It is your starting point for obtaining information. How will customers find out about you? The Internet and the breadth of information it makes available affects many daily decisions for people of all ages and in all socioeconomic groups. Thus, it can allow people and customers to keep up with changes and new information about you. There should be a seamless integration with your personal brand and the Internet.

Not only are consumers becoming more and more computer literate, but they seem more willing to risk purchasing new products and services. Customers who want to utilize your service also want to analyze your abilities and your skill without expending a lot of time. Consumers may navigate through thousands of other choices before they encounter your brand. The current business environment operates at digital speed; your brand requires that you live in that environment. If you are unable to keep up with the speed of business and its technological advances, how will your brand be positioned in the minds of potential customers? Being cutting edge doesn't mean that you spend absurd amounts of money on non-value added technology and equipment. How many successful brands are slow to react? In today's fast-paced business environment, brands don't have time to react, but to act, and to act fast. That job, that business opportunity, that business contract will not wait for you.

Digital Strategy

As the state of business has changed, so have the toys and tools that are utilized to develop and communicate their message. Today cell phones, lap tops, PDAs, and portable media devices have Wi-Fi or are web enabled. You can review and send e-mail, receive faxes, conduct web meetings, and take part in conference calls with relative ease. You can conduct web/audio conferencing without investing in audio/video conference equipment.

New media and technology allow Brand YU'ers to organize and improve the way they do business. The digital age forces you to have a global mindset and a digital strategy. Change is not an option, it is a requirement.

In the digital age, everything happens in real time; distance and time are eliminated. Real-time and web transactions allow you and your brand to travel anywhere without moving from your desk. Without a real-time mindset, you inhibit the level of effectiveness you can reach.

If you feel like you're lagging behind the newest technology and don't quite know how to begin getting up to speed, consider taking a class or two. Go online and review web sites and forums that discuss the latest technologies. Make sure you stay on top of what's happening in your field and in technology.

As the tools of the workplace change and technology changes the workplace, the places where work gets done have also changed. Today, "the office" can be anywhere, from a hammock in one's backyard to 30,000 feet up en route from one major city to the next. The following table briefly identifies the transformation in workplaces.

Traditional Workspaces	vs.	Workspaces Today
• Cubicles • Corporate offices	comparison	• Home office • Airport lounge • The beach • Wi-Fi hotspots • Coffee shops

Technology and your brand. Successfully use multiple channels to market your products, and ensure that your customers can easily and efficiently find the information they need. Two of the "hot" channels right now are blogs and podcasts.

Blogs

"Blog" is short for "Web log" and refers to an online journal that contains the writer's thoughts and comments. Blogs often contain links to other blogs or articles. Blogs are frequently updated and usually allow for comments and discussion from site visitors. Presenting a first-person point of view, well written blogs have the feel of a real conversation. Journal entries are usually chronological, starting with the most recent entry. Blogs provide real-time input from their target audience. Corporations, which are constantly trying to refine their relationships and build brand loyalty among their customers, are beginning to use blogging as a way to reach potential customers and build brand awareness.

A blog can be an excellent tool to establish yourself as a subject matter expert who is willing to assist site visitors with information on a particular product, industry, or market niche. The idea is for visitors to rely on your expertise. This reliance yields Brand YU loyalty. If you decide to blog, do your best to maintain control of the blog and steer the conversation to a positive flow. Make sure you address any brand concerns immediately and with honesty. Remember that an irate customer can turn a pleasant blog into a source of ill will. The two major types of blogs are commercial and non-commercial.

- Through a commercial blog a corporate brand gains popularity with customers through an expanded presence and by presenting a forum for the exchange of views on a particular topic.

- A non-commercial blog is generally run by a single individual who shares his or her views on a given topic or theme.

Podcasts

Podcasting is the method of distributing multimedia files, such as audio programs or music videos, over the Internet, for playback on iPods, other mobile devices, and personal computers. In laymen's terms, a podcast is a radio show in mp3 format. People can subscribe to your podcast and download it as often as they like. Content can be created in the comfort of your home with inexpensive software, a laptop or computer, and a headset microphone. It is a powerful tool that everyday people can use. One of the most popular distribution centers of podcasts is itunes.com.

How Business Gets Done

Technology is changing how business gets done. The following chart shows some the technological advancements in business tools.

Old School	vs.	New School
• Resume • Yellow pages • Newspaper • Paper planners • Paper file management • Standard mail • Next-day service	comparison	• Web presence • Google • Blogs/podcasts • PDA • Web-based solutions • E-mail • Real-time transactions

Technology Plan

To ensure the success of your brand, it is essential that you have access to and understand the latest technology. Begin by:

- Identifying what software, hardware, and telecommunications resources you need to mobilize your brand.

- Determining how to get the greatest proficiency in the shortest time possible, whether through in-class learning, a web-based tutorial, or through the help of a tutor.

- Learning to use relevant technology and web-based applications and software that allow you to take advantage of opportunities.

Daily Download

Exercise #12: Create a profile in an online job
search (e.g. monster.com,
careerbuilders.com, etc.)

Completed ☐

"Get your feet off my desk, get out of here, you stink, and we're not going to buy your product."

—Joe Keenan, President of Atari, in 1976 responding to Steve Jobs' offer to sell him rights to the new personal computer he and Steve Wozniak developed.

07°

Bring your future into the present and step towards your destiny.

"Effective leadership is not about making speeches or being liked; leadership is defined by results not attributes."

—Peter Drucker, author, The Essential Drucker

Leadershift

"It's not enough that we do our best.
Sometimes we have to do what's required."
   —*Sir Winston Churchill,*
   British Prime Minister during World War II

"Leadership development" and "leadership practices" are buzzwords that are often misused, misunderstood, and misappropriated. I did a Google search on the word *leadership* and I found 278,000,000 results. Which tells me a few things: There is a lot of information, theories, philosophies, and ideas on what leadership is and what it looks like. According to an article in *U.S. News and World Report* on America's best leaders, two-thirds of Americans say the country is in a leadership crisis.

Why? There are 6.5 billion people on the planet. There is no lack of people to be leaders; there is no lack of leadership positions for people to operate in; there is no lack of titles (even though titles don't equal leadership); there is no lack of companies or organizations to lead; there is no lack of people who need to be led; and there is no lack of problems that need to be solved or issues that need to be addressed. Then why is there a lack of true leadership? True leadership is misunderstood.

What is *Leadershift?* Leadershift is an adjustment in attitude, judgment, and emphasis that focuses on integrity-based leadership. Developing a personal brand and being a good corporate citizen, one who is responsible, responsive, and accountable is essential to success. There comes a point when every leader has to be accountable, look within, and make a shift. To shift is to change the place, position, or direction that you are going in. Life is about being able to operate at more than one speed. There comes a point when a leader has to accelerate, downshift, or turn at a moment's notice. Imagine driving a Lamborghini Zona Roadster with 18-inch wheels, a six-speed manual that goes 0–60 miles per hour in 4.0 seconds, but being unable to shift gears. You have the power at your disposal but you can't punch it at the right time. The concept of leadershift goes beyond having the equipment and tools to be a great leader; it's about utilizing what you have at the right time.

Shift to Now

Leaders operate in the now, focus on bringing their future into the present, and step toward their destiny. They understand that there may be a precise point in time to which they will never be able to return regardless of how much money or influence they have. The shift to now is about being there, being fully engaged in your mission. Many of us never get to the now because of circumstance, conditions, or difficulties we face. But although there are no perfect people or perfect brands, there are many people with the potential to perfect their brand through smart and effective decisions. The shift to now is a way to bring the complete you into the present— the project, the company, or the businesses you are engaged in.

Leadershift is about awakening the leader within you. Have you taken the steps that are required to make you a brand leader? Strong personal brands are developed by individuals who have developed strong values and character. Developing your brand leads you to a brighter future while you make your way in the current environment. Your future and your success are not dependent on conditions you can't control. Instead, it's up to you to work within whatever conditions you face and to make the necessary shifts to keep you ahead of the competition and in the forefront of your field. When is the time for leadershift? The time is now. The future is waiting for you. Go beyond fears, limitations, and boundaries and build confidence in yourself and your brand. Keep developing your leadership ability to meet your brand's needs and to meet the ever-changing needs of your market. The lifestyle of an organization's leadership directly impacts the direction and future of the organization. The character of a leader can't be separated from his or her brand. Therefore, you must always live your true calling with integrity and a true sense of responsibility. In essence, your brand and your lifestyle become inseparable. There is no end of the personal brand and beginning of you; they are one and the same.

Character development at lower ranks is required prior to elevation to higher ranks. Elevation without proper internal development will expose or reveal any flaws in the character of the leader or short-circuit future opportunities. Leadershift focuses on internal development in the early stages of your personal brand's life, when the risk and cost of exposure is lower. Late development will mean that there is a higher price to pay because there is more at risk. Internal development at all levels and stages of a brand's life cycle is not optional, it is required for sustained growth.

Shifting to now is about getting to a place where you have sustainability in operating your brand at a high level. It means more than arriving; it means maintaining and maximizing the success you achieve.

What is success? Success. . .

- is a series of good decisions.
- has nothing to do with feelings.
- is inward development exposed.
- matures with time.

Brand YU is about bringing value-added features and skills to the surface. In previous chapters we discussed development of your core, the development of who you are on the inside. Your true story lies beneath the surface. As long as it stays there it won't be read; others won't be influenced by you and what you are capable of, and your station in life won't change. As you immerse yourself in the development of your personal brand, through practice and repetition, you will grow more comfortable with having your core rise to the surface where it can be visible to and accessible by others.

Brand Stewardship

True leadership starts with an understanding of stewardship. Stewardship is about managing, supervising, and accounting for your own talents and resources and the talents and resources of others. Stewardship is the new face of leadership. A stewardship mindset is one in which the leader is more concerned about the well-being of others and respecting people regardless of their position, status, or title. As a stewardship-oriented leader, you will view any project or position as though it were your own. Imagine that your management trusts you with a project, sees you approaching it as if it is your own, observes you devoting 100 percent of your talent to methodically completing the project. That level of stewardship creates confidence in you and opportunities for you. A stewardship mindset allows you to become such an invaluable resource that your clients, employer, and colleagues will strive to maintain your involvement in their enterprise, even in lean times, because you will be seen as simply too valuable to lose. Conversely, when times are flush, you will likely be among the first to be promoted, because commitment like yours will be valued and viewed as an asset to the enterprise. Developing a set of guiding principles will help your brand flourish and become recognized for its excellence and integrity.

> **"I have not failed. I've just found**
> **10,000 ways that won't work."**
> —*Thomas Edison, American inventor*

Now that you are a passionate, mission-minded person, who has counted the cost and created your brand, you will become a person who has a developed core that is authentic, you will want to share what you have learned with someone else. You should want someone else to have it easier than you had it. Now that you have completed the personal branding process, you are responsible for identifying someone whom you can guide in developing his or her brand. The best way to validate that you understand the principles is to teach them to someone else.

The Value of Your Minute

It is time to build an authentic, meaningful brand that has integrity, that is accountable, and that embodies your values and convictions. Personal branding is about adding value. Thus, I would like to close with this thought: What is the value of your minute? Recently, I listened to a speaker who discussed the value of a minute:

- Halle Berry makes $30 a minute.
- Tiger Woods makes $175 a minute.
- Steven Spielberg makes $675 a minute.
- Bill Gates makes $6,750 a minute.

This list of well known people have invested time to become who they are and to increase their value. It's time for you to create value. Remember that you will become more of whatever you invest your time in which directly impacts your value. Life is a series of moments. Those moments make up minutes. These minutes convert to value. What is the value of your minute?

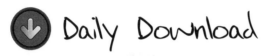 Daily Download

> **Exercise #13: Identify three people with whom you will share the information in this book.**
>
> 1. _____ ☐
>
> 2. _____ ☐
>
> 3. _____ ☐

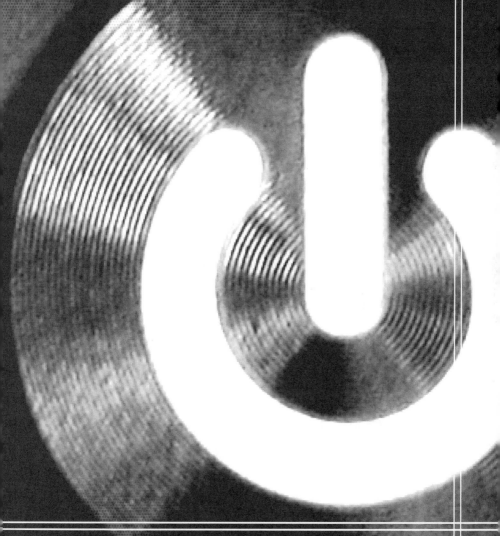

THE END.

Time to start.

Notes

Introduction

Chris Anderson (July 2006). "People Power," *Wired Magazine.*

Jeff Howe (June 2006). "The Rise of Crowdsourcing," *Wired Magazine.*

Daniel H. Pink (2001). *Free Agent Nation: The Future of Working for Yourself.* New York: Warner Business Books.

Chapter 1: Under the Influence

MacMinute (March 11, 2004). "iPod Advertising in Toronto Subway," http://www.macminute.com/2004/03/11/toronto.

Robert Berner, David Kiley, Mara Der Hovanesian, Ian Rowley, and Michael Arndt (August 1, 2005) "Global Brands", *BusinessWeek.*

Chapter Two: Pure Passion

David McNally and Karl D. Speak (2002). Be Your Own Brand: A Breakthrough Formula for Standing Out from the Crowd. San Francisco: Berrett Koehler.

Alice M. Tybout and Tim Calkins (2005). *Kellogg on Branding.* Hoboken, NJ: John Wiley & Son, Inc.

Chapter 3: The Vision and Mission Minded Person

Laurie Beth Jones (1996). The Path: Creating Your Mission Statement for Work and for Life. New York: Hyperion

Dr. J. Victor and Catherine B. Eagan (2004). *How to Discover Your Purpose in 10 Days.* Southfield, MI: Workplace Wisdom Publishing.

Red Cross (2005). Red Cross Mission Statement.
www.redcross.org/services/volunteer/0,1082,0_421_,00.html

Jeffrey Cufaude (1999). *The Character of Your Leadership,
Association Management.* Washington, D.C.

Chapter 4: XL

Kathryn D. Cramer and Hank Wasiak (2006). Change the Way
You See Everything: Through Asset-Based Thinking. Philadelphia:
Running Press.

"Play-doh." Wikipedia: The Free Encyclopedia. 09 October 2006
<http://en.wikipedia.org/wiki/Play_doh>.

"Alex Tew." Wikipedia: The Free Encyclopedia. 09 October 2006
<http://en.wikipedia.org/wiki/Alex_Tew>.

Chapter 5: Timing

Peter F. Drucker (2004). The Daily Drucker: 366 Days of Insight
and Motivation for Getting the Right Things Done. New York:
Collins.

Chapter 6: Financial Integrity

Davis Bushnell (May 2, 2004). Firm's use of credit checks grows-
job screening tighten amid post-9/11 fears. *The Boston Globe.*
Retrieved September 23, 2005, from
http://bostonworks.boston.com/globe/articles/050204_credit.html

Chapter 7: Know Your Competition

Kevin Dehoff and Vikas Sehgal (Autumn 2006). Innovations without Borders. Strategy + Business Magazine, 56-58

Notes

Chapter 8: Communication

SWOT Analysis www.monster.com

Chapter 9: Core Components

Daniel H. Pink (2005). *A Whole New Mind: Why Right-Brainers Will Rule the Future.* New York: Riverhead Books.

Chapter 10: Brand DNA

USGA Water Resources for the United States. Safe Drinking Water Act. 2005, http://water.usgs.gov.

International Bottled Water Association. *The Facts about Bottled Water (2005).*
www.bottledwater.org/public/pdf/USAtoday_final.pdf.

Fine Waters. Bottled Water Lifestyle. 2005, www.finewaters.com/Bottled_Water/Index.asp

Wally Olins (2003). On Brand. New York: Thames and Hudson.

David A. Aaker and Erich Joachimsthaler(2000). *Brand Leadership.* New York: Free Press.

Jean-Noel Kapferer (1997). *Stratgetic Brand Management: Creating and Sustaining Brand Equity Long Term.* Dover, NH: Kogan Page.

Chapter 11: Play
Cassette Tape (font): www.levilive.ro/index.html (Delarge Font)

Chapter 12: Digital Age

Chris Murray (2006). The Marketing Gurus. New York: Portfolio.

Pew/Internet (2005). Pew Internet & American Life Project. 2005, www.pewinternet.org/pdfs/PIP_Internet_and_Daily_Life.pdf.

"Play-doh." Wikipedia: The Free Encyclopedia. 09 October 2006 <http://en.wikipedia.org/wiki/Play_doh>.

Reading List

Matthew Miller and Tatiana Serafin (October 2006). "Forbes 400: The Richest People in America 2006 Edition." *Forbes Magazine*

Kevin Caroll (2004). *Rules of the Red Rubber Ball: Find and Sustain Your Life's Work.* New York: ESPN Books.

Chris Anderson (2006). *The Long Tail: Why the Future of Business Is Selling Less of More.* New York: Hyperion.

Peter F. Drucker (2001). *The Essential Drucker: The Best of Sixty Years of Peter Drucker's Essential Writings on Management.* New York: Harper Business Books.

Malcolm Gladwell (2005). *Blink: The Power of Thinking Without Thinking.* New York: Little, Brown and Company.

Dr. J. Victor and Catherine B. Eagan (2004). *How to Discover Your Purpose in 10 Days.* Southfield, MI: Workplace Wisdom Publishing.

Daniel H. Pink (2001). Free Agent Nation: The Future of Working For Yourself. New York. Warner Books.

Kevin Roberts (2004). Lovemarks: The Future Beyond Brands. New York. PowerHouse Books.

Keith Yamashita and Sandra Spataro, Ph.D. (2004). Unstuck: A Tool for Yourself, Your Team, and Your World. New York. Penguin Books.

Seth Godin (2006). Small is the new big: and 183 other riffs, rants, and remarkable business ideas. New York. Penguin Books.

LaurieBeth Jones (1996). The Path: Creating Your Mission Statement for Work and for Life. New York. Hyperion.

Photo Credits

pp. x-xi copyright istockphotos.com/pdtnc (red arrow)

p. xii copyright istockphotos.com/halfshag (boots)

p. xiii copyright istockphotos.com/ (remote)

p. xiii copyright istockphotos.com/nicalfc (pill)

p. xv copyright Beverly Rogers

p. 21 copyright istockphotos.com/Angelafoto (passion plate)

p. 37 copyright Clif Bar

pp. 40-41 copyright istockphotos.com/Angelika (subway)

p. 49 copyright istockphotos.com/ Tashka (airport sign)

p. 52 copyright istockphotos.com/sartriano (broken glasses)

p. 64 copyright istockphotos.com/KMITU (XL)

pp. 68-69 copyright istockphotos.com/zeroarmy (building)

p. 73 copyright Ernest Kim

pp. 74-75 copyright Ernest Kim

p. 77 copyright Ernest Kim

p. 85 copyright istockphotos.com/ (Ben Franklin)

p. 89 copyright istockphotos.com/ronen (watch)

pp. 94-95 copyright istockphotos.com/essxboy (financials)

p. 101 copyright istockphotos.com/ (microphone)

p. 107 copyright istockphotos.com/hidesy (hispanic man)

p. 108 copyright istockphotos.com/pattersonminx (grandma)

p. 109 copyright istockphotos.com/gisele (black woman)

p. 113 copyright istockphotos.com/PhotoEuphoria (little girl)

p. 123 copyright istockphotos.com/sdourado (weights)

p. 130 copyright istockphotos.com/selensergen (sticky notes)

pp. 132-133 copyright istockphotos.com/nikkormat42 (classroom)

p. 135 copyright istockphotos.com/PhotographerOlympus (flower)

p. 135 copyright istockphotos.com/otto_pro (ostrich)

p. 136 copyright istockphotos.com/Queeste (living room)

p. 136 copyright istockphotos.com/StanRohrer (Ford)

p. 144 copyright istockphotos.com/ (water)

p. 152 copyright istockphotos.com/Breecedownunder (meter)

p. 153 copyright istockphotos.com/jrroman (mannequin)

p. 154 copyright istockphotos.com/nostroom (tape)

p. 155 copyright istockphotos.com/kencameron (retro joystick)

p. 156 copyright istockphotos.com/InCommunicado (road block)

p. 157 copyright istockphotos.com/THEPALMER (gold fish)

p. 158-159 copyright istockphotos.com/Tiniiiii (toothpaste)

p. 160 copyright istockphotos.com/petech (photocopy)

p. 161 copyright istockphotos.com/SilentWolf (mini)

p. 162 copyright istockphotos.com/Artzone (different)

p. 163 copyright istockphotos.com/spanglish (notepad)

pp. 170-171 copyright istockphotos.com/ (digital print)

p. 177 copyright istockphotos.com/Scrofula (shift)

p. 185 copyright istockphotos.com/Brad77 (start)

p. 194 Marco Antonio (bio photo)

p. 195 copyright Hajj Flemings (Equator)

author
speaker
trainer
"I help people live their dreams."
—The Brand Man
For training or
speaking engagements.
Call 734-468-0854

Contact me

@

- www.HajjFlemings.com
- www.myspace.com/HajjEFlemings
- speak@HajjFlemings.com
- www.youtube.com/HFlemings
- www.linkedin.com/in/HajjFlemings
- www.facebook.com/people/Hajj_E_Flemings/504160425

Brand Notes

Brand Notes

Hajj E. Flemings Brand Strategist